"It's refreshing to read this ca[...]ed career and life challenges to [...]try leader and one of Canada's top consultants, Tom shares a deeply personal narrative and equally deep understanding of what it means for a consultant to practice self awareness."

-Dave Hardy RPP, President, Hardy Stevenson and Associates Limited, Executive Director, Institute for New Suburbanism

"This is a must read for those who hope to manage the next generation."

-Catherine Lyons, Partner with Goodmans LLP

"Tom provides us with deep, practical insights, borne out of his experiences, for those committed to leading successful consulting firms in any industry... His writing reflects his ongoing commitment to relationships – both with his employees and with his clients. This, his authenticity, integrity, curiosity and never-ending openness to innovate and make a difference, are hallmarks of this remarkable leader."

-Doreen E Harvey, MBA, Human Resources Consultant

A cogent, grounded examination of business practices... an engaging read. Although he primarily addresses his fellow environmental consultants, both the topics and the advice are broadly applicable across the business world. It's concisely and coherently written... Hilditch is a qualified and convincing advocate for the concept, and he makes it clear that being authentic on the job doesn't conflict with delivering solid financial results."

-Kirkus Reviews

Becoming an Enlightened Consultant

Awakened by Cancer

Tom Hilditch

◆ FriesenPress

One Printers Way
Altona, MB R0G 0B0
Canada

www.friesenpress.com

Published by Colucent Media Inc.
Cover Design by Vernon Creative Studio

ISBN
978-1-5255-9626-1 (Hardcover)
978-1-5255-9625-4 (Paperback)
978-1-5255-9627-8 (eBook)

1. Business & Economics, Consulting

Distributed to the trade by The Ingram Book Company

About the Cover
The Solar Eclipse

During a solar eclipse the moon blocks out the light of the sun. The eclipse immerses all of us in darkness leaving us without a shining path forward. After spending several months in the dark, wrestling with a significant cancer battle, I knew that the darkness would pass and that the light would once again enter and illuminate my life. The image selected for this book reminds us that when we emerge into the light, we will be stronger contributors in all that we do.

Table of Contents

Dedication

I dedicate this book to my supportive, loving, and generous family, Terry, Jaime, and Jack.

I would also like to dedicate this book to the many talented and caring teams at Hamilton Health Sciences, particularly Hamilton General Hospital and Juravinski Hospital and Cancer Centre.

Going through the experience of being diagnosed with central nervous system lymphoma, followed by surgery, chemotherapy, a stem cell transplant, and radiation, has changed my outlook on and approach to life.

To the tireless professionals who were involved in my care and recovery, both directly and behind the scenes, I want you to know how grateful I am for your care and compassion.

As such, it is with humility and gratitude that I donate a portion of the proceeds from the sale of this book to Hamilton Health Sciences Foundation.

Acknowledgements

I am grateful for the edits and ideas that Joan Hyatt (Jericho Counselling Services) provided me with on my manuscript. Joan has known me for many years and has been an anchor in the evolution of our family. I also acknowledge two other individuals who have contributed to my personal awakening, Kelly Benoit (https://www.kellybenoit.com) and Sylvia Plester-Silk (https://onpurposetransformations.ca).

Preamble

AFTER FORTY YEARS OF WORKING IN THE CONSULTING INDUSTRY, I have learned a great deal about the business and even more about myself.

I decided to create this book during the first prolonged quiet time that I have taken over the course of my career. It wasn't planned, however; this forced free time was the result of being diagnosed with cancer, a challenge that also coincided with some of the world's most difficult times. I began writing as the global pandemic (COVID-19) was emerging and accelerating its spread. As I write this now, the pandemic has resulted in more than two hundred eighty-eight million cases and more than five million deaths around the world. Along with the pandemic, burdened health care systems, and exhausted front-line workers, the global financial systems are experiencing a high level of uncertainty and volatility. Stress and anxiety levels are boiling up, and a massive movement has begun to shake racism and colonization to their roots. These rapidly emerging challenges and changes are reflected in the following chapters of Part One.

Becoming an Enlightened Consultant carefully considers the lessons, trends, and enlightened approaches to consulting that will enable individuals and firms to emerge from this transformative period and become more viable and sustainable over time.

At their core, consultants who complete sound, intelligent, and innovative work with integrity will always lead in the industry. Similarly, firms with honest and empathetic leaders will continue to outperform their competitors. And individuals and companies that choose to move away from a state of blissful ignorance toward self-awareness and enlightenment will be more successful.

Firms that choose to remain driven by egoic thinking and ignorant of their collective self-awareness and the self-awareness levels of their staff will be relegated to a declining share of their market, decreased profitability, and a steady, and in some cases rapid, increase in staff-turnover rates.

The clients of enlightened firms will respond well to the achievement of positive, effective, and more meaningful outcomes.

The environmental consulting industry, the branch of consulting that I am most familiar with, is about 50 years old. What began principally in response to emerging environmental legislation and regulations has evolved into a diverse industry with thousands of companies involved in some or all aspects of the environment (e.g., earth and life sciences, air quality, cultural considerations, socioeconomic components).

I believe that many of the messages and ideas in this book will resonate across the broader consulting industry. There are many commonalities across consulting firms and consultants who provide a range of services, including financial, accounting, management, engineering, legal, planning, and environmental, and who operate across market sectors, including private, public, Indigenous peoples/nations, and nongovernmental organizations (NGOs).

This book discusses some key elements that will help individuals and companies become well placed in and better contributors to the consulting industry and to the communities in which they work. It helps to define how self-awareness and enlightenment will globally transform the consulting industry and society in general. The coming era will markedly change the consulting industry, including who the dominant players are and how operations and outcomes will evolve. This transformation is long overdue.

PART ONE

AS I REFLECTED MORE DEEPLY ON MY EXPERIENCE IN THE CONSULTING industry and my journey recovering from cancer, I realized that the book I wanted to write really comprised two major, interrelated pieces. I chose to create Part One and Part Two to make reading and understanding the information clearer and simpler.

Part One explores how individuals and companies can develop their individual and collective self-awareness and move towards enlightened outcomes. While it touches on all of the key aspects of consulting, Part One looks at these aspects from an evolutionary perspective, offering observations and ideas related to trends in the consulting industry and where the most important opportunities and transformations are taking place.

I believe that Part One contains the most important information about how a transformation is underway in some more aware companies and to a lesser degree in the broad consulting industry. Part Two includes a number of more detailed observations regarding the state of today's consulting industry and, in particular, about the markets and clients. It also incorporates some more information about the environmental consulting industry, including the types of projects and services that I have encountered over my career and the types of clients with whom I have worked. I offer some detailed observations about working with Indigenous peoples, the movement towards decolonization, and the role of environmental nongovernmental organizations (ENGOs).

If you have the time, I suggest you read both parts in the order presented.

Chapter 1

Introduction—
Why This Book and Why Now?

I NEARLY DIED IN THE FALL OF 2019. THIS BOOK AROSE DURING ONE OF the most challenging periods of my life.

On July 4, 2019, I was diagnosed with a brain tumour. On August 27, ninety percent of the cancerous mass was surgically removed. Less than a week later, I was admitted to the hematology ward at the Juravinski Hospital to receive a regimen of chemotherapeutic drugs, known as the Matrix. My tumour, according to the biopsy report, was an aggressive and rare form of blood cancer, also known as central nervous system lymphoma. The good news was that it was curable. The goal was to get the cancer into remission in eight months.

My remission-targeted journey included awake brain surgery; time in the intensive-care and cardiac-care units; an emergency hospital stay due to a serious blood infection; four sessions of chemotherapy, each requiring five days of hospitalization; stem-cell harvesting; additional chemotherapy prior to the reinfusion of my stem cells; and some low-dose precautionary radiation. News came to me on December 24, 2019—Christmas Eve—that my cancer was in remission, four months ahead of schedule.

My cancer journey was the closest I have come to facing my mortality. My family didn't know where this journey was headed when I became non-responsive, post brain surgery. I've heard of near-death experiences leading to changes and transformations in people; now I can identify with them. I have emerged a changed person: intellectually, emotionally, physically, and spiritually.

I used some of my treatment and recovery time to think about my life, and specific to this book, to reflect on my forty-year career in the consulting industry. My personal transformation occurred in parallel with a global awakening and a widespread call for transformative changes in many aspects of our world (e.g., the need for racial and economic equity, reformation of deeply distorted and self-interested politics, and a wholesale change in how we manage and interact with nature).

To set the context and to share a little bit about myself, let me begin this story a bit further back.

I graduated from the University of Guelph in 1981 with a Bachelor of Science in Resources Management. My graduation coincided with a recession in Canada. It was a period of high inflation, soaring interest rates, and substantial unemployment. I graduated in May of that year. By August, the Bank of Canada interest rate hit 20%, and the inflation rate averaged more than 12%. During the economic collapse of the early 1980s, the unemployment rate jumped, increasing from 7.6% in 1981 to about 12.0% in 1983. It was not an ideal time for a new grad to be heading into the workplace. Today's graduates must feel quite challenged, as they seek out their entry positions in an economy that has been disrupted by sectoral lags and collapses due to the COVID-19 pandemic.

Undeterred, in 1981 I decided to create my own consulting firm and move forward, expecting better times ahead. I founded Panax Resources Management with no consulting experience. I simply chose to believe that I could make a successful go of it. I still vividly remember how excited I was to hand design my first business card and to begin to look for work. That was during a time, long before desktop publishing, when we all depended upon Letraset's dry rub-down, instant lettering methods. That was also a time before fax machines, mobile phones, and word-processing technologies.

A naïve soul then, I decided to approach the leader of one of Canada's principal environmental consulting firms for advice—I was sure its president would want to help me understand how to successfully create a competing firm. Instead of guidance, he offered me a job on the spot, which I eagerly (and gratefully) accepted. I was the sole member of my graduating class to get a job in the environmental field that year.

I was excited to begin consulting, and my career developed along a path that saw me help to grow two well-known firms from about 30 staff to approximately 150 staff each. I stayed with each firm for about a dozen years, moving rapidly up the ranks from a junior ecologist, to ownership, to executive-leadership levels, while simultaneously maintaining and enhancing my technical expertise. I developed a depth of knowledge around operating and growing a business, investing much of my energy in strategic thinking and learning about all aspects of marketing and sales. I have participated in the sale and purchase of consulting firms and led the integration of teams during post-merger and acquisition periods. I have been a senior leader in larger firms with between 900 and 10,000 people, and I have personally led teams comprising between 10 and 250 members. Perhaps more importantly, I have worked on hundreds of interesting and challenging projects alongside a diversity of clients and regulators who have expressed their opinions from both optimistic and cynical perspectives.

After investing 25 years of my career helping to grow and lead firms where I had a minority but growing level of ownership, I decided it was time for me to start fresh and create a new firm that would better reflect my interests and values. So, in 2006, I established Savanta Inc. I wanted to create a firm that would contribute to better outcomes for clients. Our website explained:

> We are known for finding innovative solutions to difficult environmental and approval challenges. Our specialized natural heritage technical expertise, leading capabilities in socio-economic and climate change work, and our out-of-the-box thinking help us achieve desired outcomes for our clients. We work collaboratively amongst various stakeholders, turning away from the common reflex reaction to settle into polarized positions. We continue to successfully attract clients and staff that share this vision and approach to business.

> Savanta is committed to effective engagement, building community trust in a project's ability to balance environmental, social, and technical components and in its ability to maximize community benefits. We take on any number of roles, depending upon project complexity and characteristics. In addition, we are accustomed to serving as strategic advisors and facilitating regulatory approvals on complex files. Savanta is an environmental consulting firm that doesn't shy away from testing existing rules and practices where they no longer serve to generate intelligent and meaningful outcomes.

> Our diverse team listens first, thinks differently, and is passionate about balancing environmental, economic, and social needs to create better, more intelligent outcomes.

As I built Savanta to a team of 40, we managed to achieve some interesting, exciting, and meaningful outcomes. Starting a firm from scratch presents an opportunity to create and deliver upon a thoughtful vision that could be quite different from a typical or traditional consulting firm. I learned early on that independent, boutique-type firms can be more innovative, nimble, resilient, and profitable.

I'm now heading into my fortieth year in the consulting industry, and I'm not finished yet. Over the past four decades, my focus has been on impact assessment, mitigation planning and design, and ecological planning and restoration (which I personally refer to as "rewilding"). I've led hundreds of environmental assignments, including coastal zone and regional landscape planning in China, Venezuela, and Barbados. In Canada, where the bulk of my experience has been, I have worked on major resource and infrastructure impact assessments (e.g., mineral aggregate quarries, landfills, toxic-waste disposal facilities, nuclear and renewable energy projects) and development studies (e.g., new urban communities). In addition, I've provided expert testimony and have been tested by lawyers, including panels of lawyers, at dozens of hearings and tribunals.

I have presented scientific papers to large and small audiences around the world. I am recognized for my strong verbal and written communication skills and for being thoughtful, articulate, and persuasive. But I'm perhaps best known for my positive and collaborative approach to projects and for my interest in reaching practical and meaningful outcomes. I tend to think differently than most consultants, always looking to understand issues and projects from multiple perspectives. As a middle child, the peace broker, I think I was trained early on to lead people to mutually acceptable and constructive solutions. I have learned that thinking differently is a fundamental part of differentiating individuals and their companies from competitors.

In 2015, I was appointed by the Government of Ontario to serve as chair of the Committee on the Status of Species at Risk in Ontario; I continue to serve in that role. That appointment followed my service on a sister committee: the Species at Risk Program Advisory Committee from 2008 to 2014. Late in 2020 I was appointed to serve on the Board of Directors with the Anishinabek/Ontario Fisheries Resource Centre.

One of the most meaningful experiences I have enjoyed in consulting came with my appointment by the Henvey Inlet, Shawanaga, and Magnetawan First Nations in Canada to serve as their environmental stewardship commissioner. In that capacity, I provided oversight and compliance auditing associated with environmental permitting for a 300-megawatt renewable wind energy facility on Indigenous lands. That project woke me up to better understanding and exploring my personal and corporate relationships with Indigenous peoples. It also helped me to understand and acknowledge the privileged position I hold in relation to many individuals and communities.

In mid-2018, I decided that it was time to sell Savanta to use deeper pockets to scale it up. I interacted with a few international firms who were interested and decided to enter into negotiations with one of them. Later in this book, I offer more about the decision to sell. In January 2019, I sold the company, a fortuitous move given I was diagnosed with cancer five months later. I remain deeply grateful for the skilled team I helped to grow over Savanta's 13-year independent life. They stepped up in my absence to perform as mature, skilled, and confident consultants.

Today, I continue to create new consulting firms; it seems once an entrepreneur, always an entrepreneur.

Chapter 2

Self-Awareness and Enlightenment— Meaning and Impacts

WHILE I WASN'T COMPLETELY SURE WHAT SELF-AWARENESS MEANT, IT sounded reasonable to me that I must be self-aware. I'm an intelligent person and a successful consultant/business owner—of course I'm self-aware.

My cancer gave me a rare gift of time to stop and reflect and to read voraciously about topics I'm interested in and curious about. My "References and Helpful, Inspiring Resources" section at the back of this book lists a sampling from my library that I excitedly and insatiably consumed while completing research for this book.

As I read, I began to realize what the term self-awareness actually meant. In its simplest form, self-awareness means having a conscious knowledge of your character, feelings, motives, and desires. The term conscious points towards the need to separate and observe your ego as one aspect of your self. Each of us is different; we have our own backgrounds and perspectives and yet we share so much in common. As I have become more self-aware, I have begun to understand our shared experiences and shared origins more deeply. We may look different and practise different belief systems, but we all share a common humanity. We also have our own egos, the voices in our heads that tend to lead us in our own directions.

As I looked more objectively at some of the conversations I routinely entered into and some of the interactions I have created/encountered, it became clear to me that I had more work to do to clearly understand the role that my ego played in my personal and professional life. My cancer recovery time accelerated my learning process and led to what I can only describe as a personal transformation, a level of growth that I have not previously experienced.

In Chapter 1, I referred to various roles and titles I have achieved in my consulting career. I now recognize that at points in my life, I held onto those roles and titles as an indication of who I was and how successful I had become; they defined me, or so I believed. Looking back now, after facing my mortality, I can see that cancer allowed me to begin to awaken to who I really am. I was jolted into the realization that I am much more than just the titles and positions that I have held.

The parts of my consulting life that have been most important to me were those moments when I felt that I was making a positive difference to communities and people and to nature. I realized my titles and roles were what my ego wanted me to broadcast and celebrate. I have taken this time to revisit who I am, to better understand my true purpose and how I can best support and drive positive outcomes. I acknowledge that I have spent the last few decades working intensely as a human "doing," not as a human "being." My time away from work has allowed me to think more carefully about being present in all that I do.

By nature, I'm an introvert, and my shyness, earlier in my life, limited my ability to engage in meaningful and intimate relationships. I have invested countless hours (and lots of money) in various forms of therapy trying to understand the roots of my behaviours and characteristics. I have begun to see more clearly the gifts my parents gave me in terms of their contributions to my character. I more fully understand the gift of the origins of my behaviours, for better or worse. Why am I shy, and is that good or bad? It's neither; it is what it is. There are strengths and opportunities for both introverts and extroverts.

The few colleagues to whom I have admitted my reserved nature were surprised—to them I appeared extroverted. For me, my shyness caused me to hide my true self under a different, more outgoing mask to play the various and potentially uncomfortable roles that I entered into. Acting in a manner that was in stark contrast to my natural disposition consumed a significant amount of energy and also involved and depended upon my ego. That led me into some troubled periods in my life when I struggled with anxiety, social and mood disorders, and addictions.

I have learned that my self-awareness requires an honest and objective look at my strengths, weaknesses, and values. I found that this period of introspection allowed me to objectively observe that what I had considered to be some of my strengths were, in fact, weaknesses.

For example, I thought I was decisive. I now realize that, at times, my decisiveness was an attempt by my ego to control situations. Rather than actively listening, understanding, and empowering others, I would become impatient and ready to jump in to decide simply to move things along. That's not informed decisiveness; it's my ego trying to insert itself to tell my friends and colleagues that I am right and that decisions need to flow my way, and quickly.

As I have thought more deeply about how I communicate, and as I have observed my ego more objectively and rigorously, I have become more self-aware. I am better able to recognize and manage my reactions. I now understand more distinctly how my words and actions affect other people, and I am reacting and overreacting much less than before. I am becoming more present in conversations by listening more carefully and giving matters the thought, they deserve.

I have also realized that I seem to get impatient frequently; I hadn't noticed that before. Rather than allowing people to complete tasks they were undertaking, I would too quickly step in to take some assignments back, telling myself that I believed that I could achieve better results more swiftly. It's now more obvious to me that my impatience is a reminder to me to pause, recognize and respect the work of others, and allow tasks and work to unfold more naturally. I do not need to listen to my ego telling me that I am better than someone else and that I need to control outcomes. That's the opposite of what I truly need.

I do believe that those who get to know their thought processes and behavioural patterns better are those who are more likely to be able to improve them. It's also clear that those who begin to observe their egos and egos around them will be able to contribute more meaningfully in all that they do.

Our egos are the self-identities that we have each created through our lives. In my case it's the result of six decades of pattern formation and repetition. The ego, which is neither good nor bad, is created through our thoughts. It results from and dominates the actions and behaviours of many who have not yet developed their self-awareness (Meurisse 2019). When my ego flares up and takes control of my thinking and actions, I can now see and feel that to be the case. I am able to more quickly step back from egoic thinking. I am reacting less, thinking more, and observing why and when my ego kicks in. After several months of introspection, I believe I have reached an entirely new level of awareness.

Interestingly, as I have become more self-aware, my ego seems to be desperately trying to object to my awakening, trying to push me into old patterns such as being critical and judgemental. I don't think my ego likes that I have outed it. And it doesn't like that I am recognizing and shutting down those ego-driven behaviours much more quickly.

Egoic thinking is grounded in entrenched habits of thought, enforced by societal consciousness and unconscious repetition (Jeffrey 2018). When we listen to and react (or overreact) with our egoic thinking, we can move into areas of negative thinking and energy. Operating from a negative place, such as resentment, frustration, or anger, does not help individuals or companies make better decisions or significant advancements.

Our egos often guide us into comparisons with others, which can lead to negative emotional experiences. Living in or with negative emotions can steer us to choose paths that will create unnecessary problems and resistance to better outcomes, whereas living in or with positive emotions (e.g., optimism, enthusiasm, gratitude) will allow a more natural flow of better opportunities and outcomes.

I have created a simple tool, a checklist (see Figure 1) that helps me identify when my ego is most active. It relies heavily upon and draws from the teachings of Abraham (Hicks and Hicks 2004). I use that tool daily to help me define when my ego is interfering and trying to sidetrack my intentions. When I find my thoughts becoming negative, I know that my ego is attempting to take control. I have come to believe that we should spend the majority of our personal and professional time experiencing positive emotions—those listed above the neutral line in Figure 1.

POSITIVE EMOTIONS	NEGATIVE EMOTIONS
Joyful, Appreciative, Empowered, Free, Loving	
Passionate Enthusiastic, Eager Happy Positive Expectations and Belief Optimistic Hopeful Satisfied, Content	
Feeling NEUTRAL	
if here, → *work yourself up the ladder.*	Bored
	Pessimistic
	Frustrated, Irritated Impatient Overwhelmed Disappointed Doubtful *These are places* Worried *where you will* Blameful *not work* Discouraged *productively* Angry Vengeful Hateful Jealous Insecure, Guilty, Unworthy Afraid, Fearful, Grieving, Depressed, Powerless

Figure 1: Emotional Guidance Framework

I believe that when we operate or live, in alignment with our positive emotions, we are happier and more enthusiastic and creative in all that we do. When we operate below that neutral line—i.e., when we feel overwhelmed, frustrated, discouraged, angry, or afraid—we should pause and pay careful attention to what we are thinking. Our busy minds and egos can keep us entangled in darker, less effective emotional spaces.

Eckhart Tolle (2005, 2011) speaks clearly about the role our egos play. When we find fault in others and blame people and circumstances for our perceived failings, we know our egos are active. It's our egos that cause us to criticize others, to make them seem less important than ourselves. If someone has more, knows more, or can do more, that's when our egos feel threatened. When we feel impatient, pessimistic, disappointed, or worried, it's time to pause and listen to what our negative emotions are telling us. Look inside before challenging and casting blame outside.

Egoic thinking creates resistance and is more prevalent in men than in women. Ego likes feeling right because that makes someone else wrong. An ego can live in a negative place and prefers we are not awake to its constant efforts to control our thoughts and actions. Ego demands personal recognition and wastes energy in resentment if it doesn't get enough.

So how do we manage our egos and respond differently? We need to take responsibility for our inner thoughts and regularly ask ourselves: Is there any negativity in me right now? I have begun to let go of my identification with my thoughts and have become more aware of my emotions, in real time. When I hear some of the negative and judgemental thoughts in my mind, I notice that I am observing and listening to my ego. That sounds straightforward, but I found it took some time and the wake-up call of cancer to really understand how to actively listen. I still catch myself falling into egoic thinking, albeit less frequently and less intensely.

I recall one vivid example of when my ego reacted. I was involved in litigation and was representing a private-sector client. Just before I was to stand up and testify, the opposing attorney remarked in a low voice, as I passed his seat, that he hoped I wasn't going to spread lies again. He looked up and smiled at me as I glanced down at him—I'm sure with a perplexed look on my face. His comment shook me, or more to the point, it inflamed my ego. I allowed his snide remark to throw me off my game. My ego took over and my evidence did not go well. I was left questioning why he would utter such derogatory words. I have deliberately avoided any interactions with him for the remaining years of my career. Egos can be disruptive and manipulative. It's only when I remember my truth that I can deflect such negative energy.

I have invested much time in quiet reflection and in both silent and guided meditation. These efforts have helped me not only to slow the thoughts racing through my head, but to also be open to considering guidance that will help me make better decisions. I remain on track most of the time but still observe old patterns and behaviours trying to re-emerge.

How I react to people and situations, especially when challenges arise, is the best indicator of how deeply I know myself. As I have become more self-aware, I do not hear misleading statements, exaggerated opinions, and criticisms from others as personal offenses. I have learned to observe that their behaviours and remarks are most often more about them, not about me. And over time, as I choose not to react to them, others' egos will not invest time and energy in me. When ignored or worked around, I observe that egos cannot gain the energy needed through negative inter-actions and emotions.

Regardless of most situations, I now choose to respond with kindness towards others. This allows me to act in a manner that reflects a true strength of character. I am humbled to recognize how important every-one is and how we are not better or worse than one another—we are essentially the same. Humility and a sense of humbleness naturally exude from those who awaken to better understand themselves.

Having explored and begun to deepen my own self-awareness, it seems more apparent than ever that improved self-awareness and a shift towards enlightenment will lead to more effective and meaningful consulting careers and companies.

When considering the term enlightenment for this book, I found myself investigating many resources, including the Golden Rule in Christianity and the five main teachings of Buddhism. I also turned to read and re-read books by other business and wisdom and spirituality teachers for guidance (e.g., Lencioni, Drucker, Gladwell, Covey, Tolle, Dyer, Chopra, Gray, Dispenza).

Enlightenment means different things to different people. Enlightenment is a term applied to a movement in Europe from about 1650 to 1800, which advocated the use of reason and individualism instead of tradition and established doctrine. In Hinduism and Buddhism, enlightenment is referred to as a state of attaining spiritual knowledge or insight, characterized by the elimination of desire and suffering.

Why choose the word enlightenment in this book? To continue to promote an important dialogue about the larger context within which we all operate. I believe that we are all here on purpose, and we are meant to create and co-create better outcomes. According to some spiritual teachers and authors (Tolle 2005, 2011; Dyer 2012), we are meant to live joyful lives. We may not understand that completely yet, as our individual and collective understanding depends upon where each of us is on our journey towards self-awareness.

I have read many books about business and many about spirituality and personal development. I had thought I was learning to become more enlightened, but it was not until this cancer recovery journey that I realized that I was only dancing on the surface of those readings. As I sifted through my ever-expanding library, I understood that simply reading these books doesn't result in self-awareness. There's much more required to objectively observe and understand, before ultimately choosing to make personal transformative changes.

I also realized that my hope with this book was to offer others some simpler and more practical examples and guidance that might support and accelerate them on their self-awareness and enlightenment trek. A cancer diagnosis is not a prerequisite to an individual's awakening. I felt an urge to try to simplify and amplify messages that others have captured so eloquently, but that cognitively seemed relatively inaccessible to more common people like me. We all have egos; we share and can benefit from simply recognizing and understanding that fact. Our awareness grows from there.

Much has been written about leadership, business, and innovation, and much has been written about spirituality, personal development/growth, and self-awareness. In few cases, however, do those paths cross, or do those ideas integrate. In some cases, more traditional business books are dismissive of deeper (or ethereal) thoughts and considerations, and sound more like efforts to make the authors appear smarter than their readers. In this book, I offer a blend of suggestions, tools, and observations gleaned from many resources combined with my experiences with a diversity of consultants and consulting firms.

Key Points and Observations in Chapter 2:

Self-Awareness and Enlightenment—
Meaning and Impacts

1. Self-awareness means having a conscious knowledge of your character. The term conscious points towards the need to separate and observe your ego as only one aspect of your self.

2. Titles and roles are what our egos want to celebrate. Taking time to understand who we really are, beyond the ego, will support and drive positive outcomes.

3. Living primarily in positive emotions will lead to the natural flow of better opportunities and outcomes.

4. To manage our egos, we need to take responsibility for our inner thoughts by regularly asking: Is there any negativity in me right now?

5. We need to move beyond dancing on the surface of important books by understanding them and by leaning into transformative actions.

6. We all have egos; we share and can benefit from simply recognizing and understanding that fact. Our awareness grows from there.

Chapter 3
The Evolving and Transforming Nature of Consulting

FIRMS THAT UNDERSTAND AND CREATE TRULY INTEGRATED AND COL-laborative trans-disciplinary teams will lead the industry. The term integration has been used extensively, but I have not had an opportunity to observe many cases where it has worked to the extent it can and should.

Integration means more than having a senior design, engineering, planning, or environmental professional bundling up and leading a team of various internal and/or external experts. It means understanding the nature of the assignment more fully and ensuring that it is properly led and implemented by an appropriate cross- and trans-disciplinary team. I chose the word trans-disciplinary because it means going beyond the more common cross- or multi-disciplinary definitions. It transcends the boundaries of various disciplines and causes us to understand more fully what is often left unanswered: the interrelationship and interactions amongst the knowledge and understanding of different disciplines.

In my world of environmental consulting, understanding the landscape means seeing it in a three-dimensional form, where everything on the surface is also connected to and dependent upon what's beneath the surface. It addresses questions such as, how does the surface water interact with ground water, and how do pathways and linkages form and persist? How do humans respond to nature, other individuals, and communities?

How can Western, Eastern, and Indigenous methods and approaches to nature be understood and translated into meaningful, complementary, and unified actions?

Fully allowing team members to respectfully provide innovative thinking and complementary contributions, without the constraints of egoic thinking or hierarchical barriers, will improve intelligent outcomes.

Early in my career, many of my consulting assignments were delivered as a sub-consultant to engineering, planning, and architectural firms. I sensed then, as I do now, that ego played an influential role in the perpetuation of the myth that only certain technical professionals are capable of leading assignments. I witnessed, for example, landscape architects who resented engineers and architects managing projects without an understanding of how to integrate built forms within a landscape, the apparent realm of landscape architects. I have also observed engineers directing projects that I believe would have been better led by planners. The list of these observations could go on. From these experiences and my more recent awakening, it has become clear to me that egos are interfering with decisions and blocking better outcomes in the consulting industry. No one discipline is superior to another and operating in isolated silos results in unintentional blindness to the helpful and alternative ideas that others express when we choose to actively listen.

In some areas and firms, egos are running rampant with the ill-informed treatment of people in many technical disciplines, specializations, and individuals. Personally, I have found that egoic people tend to flock together and protect one another from potentially becoming more informed. It's hard to visualize true collaboration and integration when these attitudes persist. Perhaps these behaviours have been instilled and reinforced by academic institutions and their leaders who stake claims around the supremacy of their professions and teachings.

Another factor that seems to block true collaboration is the dominance of privileged White men in leadership roles in consulting. In the larger firms that I have worked in, the cluster of senior White men at the top seemed intent on protecting themselves (and their egos) and using their positions of power and authority to reinforce their belief that they are better than others. (Please note that it is not my intention to lump all White men together).

The evolving marketplace is demanding true collaboration that embraces and includes a trans-disciplinary approach to consulting. This means that it is no longer acceptable for large, predominantly one-discipline-led consulting firms to "bolt on" supplementary services to deliver a project. A genuine transformation of firms and approaches in the consulting industry is required and obtainable.

The markets continue to change as the service demands shift. New, small, and specialized start-ups are rapidly becoming established, capturing emerging niche markets (e.g., climate change, sustainability, Indigenous services) and employing new approaches and technologies to business. The quest to develop more innovative and enlightened work environments in these emerging and flourishing firms will present significant barriers to businesses wishing to acquire or merge with them.

Unless driven to a sale for financial or successional reasons, many of these niche firms will choose to maintain their leading-edge cultures and continue in their specialized markets. They will likely prefer to evolve and change as rapidly as necessary, maintaining a high level of resiliency in the face of significant changes (e.g., fossil fuel decline, pandemics).

The long-established approach to increasing administrative systems (e.g., accounting, legal, invoicing, record keeping) and overhead is being challenged by emerging trends, including remote business models with limited individual or shared central offices, to fully working from home. Some of these approaches involve decreased operating costs, tax advantages to the individual team members, and more resilient, cloud-based storage systems to access centralized filing. The COVID-19 pandemic is reminding and pushing all firms, regardless of size, to explore alternatives to the traditional brick and mortar office models.

In terms of the rapidly emerging remote-based business models, consultants would be wise to now ask themselves the following questions:

- Does our work demand the floor space and number of formal offices we currently have?

- What aspects of our work need to be physically centralized (e.g., accounting, finance, legal)?

- What aspects can be centralized without physical space (e.g., cloud-based, accessible file storage)?

- What technologies can we add to enhance connectivity in a remote model?

- If we were to experiment with a remote model, are there locations where we should pilot test the approach (e.g., where leases are coming due soonest)?

- How can decentralizing and reducing our office space consumption reduce our costs and allow more strategic investments?

- How will our team members respond to a remote workspace?

- Can we trust our team members to complete their work remotely?

The last question about trust is a particularly important one to consider. If you find you have trouble trusting your team, it's time to look carefully at your own biases and perspectives. It's also time to ask yourself whether you understand and can manage your own egoic thinking. If you as a leader have trouble trusting your team members, you may have the wrong managers, leaders, and/or team members assembled to complete the work.

It's time to challenge and carefully examine how to do things differently, including the belief that the production of high-quality and integrated work requires employees to assemble in one workspace. If you are a leader and have difficulty being open-minded, then you may be relegating your operation to out-dated and stale patterns of thinking and behaviour.

When I created Savanta Inc. in 2006, I decided we would operate as a remote model, regardless of the number of employees. That was after eleven years of commuting 1.5 hours each way to an office with my former company. The new remote model allowed team members to balance their work and personal lives more effectively without unnecessary and crowded commutes to one or more central offices. I estimate that this new business model personally saved me about 600 hours (i.e., 75 days @ eight hours per day) of commuting time each year.

With the remote model, we were able to attract staff from a variety of geographies (i.e., outside traditionally accepted commuting distances), which allowed for more diverse local representation and an ability to better serve new client bases without increasing operational costs. We were seen as an early innovator that chose to place interest in the well-being of our team members and their families at the top of our agenda, alongside our commitment to professionally service the needs of our clients. This progressive approach set the stage for rapid growth and attracted team members from competing firms who were looking to continue their professional lives in a more balanced and healthy manner.

The reduction in typical operating costs associated with the remote model and positioning the firm at the high-value end of the market allowed Savanta to undertake several important practices and activities, as follows.

1. *Compensation and Benefits*
   - Paying above-average salaries.
   - Paying annual bonuses that were above industry standards.
   - Putting in place a generous benefit program with health care and personal spending accounts.
   - Adding top-ups to standard (but still generous) Canadian maternity benefits.
   - Providing financial support and salary continuance to staff and families experiencing difficult and challenging personal periods.

2. *Technological Investments*
   - Providing all team members with sophisticated hardware, software, and mobile technologies.
   - Self-investing in and developing innovative software (e.g., the Red Squirrel electronic ecology field data collection app, discussed in detail in Chapter 8).

3. *Training and Development*
   - Hiring and paying high-school and university-level interns positive and fair living wages and providing active and progressive learning opportunities.
   - Retaining experienced human resources specialists and trainers to optimize performance and learning exchange dialogues and

to increase team member self-awareness through expert guided training (e.g., Insights Discovery, Birkman Method, discussed in detail in Chapter 6).

- Funding staff engaged in post-graduate education.

4. *Branding and Positioning*

- Investing in leading-edge branding and website/social media implementation.

- Providing all team members with high-end Savanta-branded clothing.

- Translating some important information into the native language of clients and potential clients (e.g., Mandarin, Spanish).

- Attending and participating in several industry association and science-based organization events and conferences, regardless of location.

5. *Completing Independent Research*

- Investing in special, self-funded research projects (e.g., supporting the recovery of Kirtland's warbler endangered species habitat).

- Writing balanced opinion pieces and supporting technical book writing and publishing by individual employees and teams (e.g., catalogues of local flora, wetland policy critiques, guidance).

6. *Giving Back*

- Contributing to several science-based organizations and associations that were meaningful to our firm and to many of our individual team members.

- Annually contributing to science fairs to encourage youth engaged in science programs.

- Supporting causes and activities that were important to staff and their families.

- Investing in and creating a unique, sold-out Toronto conference on endangered species.

7. *Celebrating Our Advancements*

- Applauding our contributions to the industry and to the communities we worked with each year with a multi-day team member event at one of my favourite inns (Langdon Hall Country House Hotel & Spa, Cambridge, Ontario).

To a large degree, geography became irrelevant in our work. Savanta also benefitted directly by the reduction in operating costs. As a result of attracting and satisfying some of the best team members in the industry, we essentially eliminated typical costs associated with normal, annual staff-turnover rates (e.g., costs associated with advertising, hiring, training, and integrating new staff).

And team members benefitted in several ways, including

- increased workday flexibility;
- more time each day to include personal wellness and family activities;
- decreased commuting-related production of greenhouse gas emissions and decreased costs (wear and tear on vehicles, human fatigue, risks); and
- an ability to expense, against personal taxes, some household costs associated with the operation of a home office.

Our model was based upon the following core principles and practices:

Trust: We trusted team members to meet their business obligations. In return, team members recognized that we valued their hard work, well-being, and career development.

Improved and Optimized Communications: We committed to optimizing the efficiency of communications in this remote model (e.g., improved meeting-management skills). We also invested heavily in IT to allow team members to use the best Apple hardware as core business tools. In addition, we experimented with and implemented evolving connectivity technologies (e.g., video conferencing).

Increased Efficiencies: Over years of consulting, it struck me many times that meetings—including general staff meetings—tended to unnecessarily drag on and erode the effectiveness and efficiency of communications. Instead, we chose to organize efficient business/social gatherings that inspired team members.

Team Member Support: The trust and flexibility underlying this model allowed team members to reach out to one another efficiently and effectively as needed. Employees were, in most cases, clustered in smaller areas within Ontario's broad geography, facilitating easy and direct get-togethers amongst themselves (e.g., kitchen-table meetings, coffee-shop gatherings). We also chose to create a small, space-optimized collaborative workspace in a location that was reachable to all members of our team without extensive travel. That space enabled us to avoid having to pay for desk space in other firms' offices or having to pay hotel-boardroom costs on a regular basis. The space, furnishings, resources, and décor (including staff photography enlarged on canvases) were designed and equipped in a way to optimize flexibility and comfort.

Key Points and Observations in Chapter 3:

The Evolving and Transforming Nature of Consulting

1. Fully allowing team members to respectfully provide innovative thinking and contributions, without the constraints of egoic thinking or hierarchical barriers, will improve intelligent outcomes.

2. Egos are interfering with better outcomes and decisions in the consulting industry. Egos are negatively impacting many technical disciplines and specializations.

3. Firms that embrace trans-disciplinary and collaborative approaches to consulting will thrive, while larger consulting firms dominated by one discipline that periodically bolts on needed services to address specific projects will not.

4. Unless driven to a sale for financial or successional reasons, many niche firms will choose to maintain their leading-edge cultures and remain in their specialized markets.

5. It's time to challenge and carefully examine how to do things differently. If you are a leader and you have difficulty empowering and trusting your team, you may be relegating your operation to traditional and stale patterns of thinking and behaviour.

6. Today, we are presented with an opportunity for a genuine transformation of firms and approaches in the consulting industry.

7. The COVID-19 pandemic is reminding and pushing all firms, regardless of size, to explore alternatives to the traditional brick and mortar office models.

Chapter 4

Finding the Work—
A Shifting Approach to Marketing and Sales

I'VE ATTENDED MANY BOOTCAMPS AND TRAINING SESSIONS OVER THE years, addressing topics such as sales, cold calling, proposal writing, and turning leads into projects. None of those sessions referred to self-awareness or enlightenment or even to the role that our egos play in attracting clients and projects. And none of them made a lasting impression on me or improved my consulting behaviours. Perhaps I wasn't listening carefully enough, or perhaps we need to look for more authentic and less me-first sales approaches.

I believe we are entering a transformative period in the marketing and sales aspects of consulting. Fundamentally, we have an opportunity to consider sales from a different perspective. It's not important to tell clients how wonderful you are or to give them a long list of services that you can provide. And it's not appropriate to try to lure and outsmart clients; that's your and your company's collective egos talking. It's time to manage our egos far more effectively and to neutralize and displace the traditional and persistent hard-core, me-first sales approach.

Sales

It's important to understand that the term sales can and should be replaced with other more current, relevant, and appropriate terms such as knowledge and idea sharing. One experience I had resonates with me on this topic; it was a sales trip where I closed no sales but felt excited about the outcome.

On one of my early marketing trips to northern Ontario, targeted towards finding business in the mining and pulp and paper sectors, I bought all the local papers, made cold calls, and lined up meetings with prominent businesses and government agency staff. What I remember most about this sales trip, though, is not that I was unsuccessful in returning to the office with a signed contract (which was not a realistic objective), but rather that I helped potential clients find solutions to their problems without saddling them with consulting costs.

In my home community in Niagara Region, I had observed various forms of wood and paper waste being used in vineyards for soil improvement. Before heading north, I had begun thinking about and researching the potential use of lime and wood waste to increase the effectiveness of ecological restoration on areas of the rugged, acidic Canadian Shield.

Upon arrival in northern Ontario, I started the process of cold calling. Over the course of a couple of hours, I learned that a firm was having trouble disposing of wood waste while another firm had an excess supply of a by-product, lime. I introduced the two industrial companies to each other, which ultimately led to a solution that helped both achieve efficient outcomes and also helped improve the environment. A win-win-win scenario. I felt more excited about resolving a real and practical problem than trying to close on a consulting contract.

In contrast, I experienced a less inspiring and ego-driven trip to Halifax, Nova Scotia, where I attended a major environmental conference. Unfortunately, my flight from Toronto to Halifax arrived late, and I simply threw my luggage into my hotel room and went quickly to the convention level to join the dinner session, which was already in progress. I found my nametag and I peeked through a porthole-shaped window into the room, filled with I would estimate to be a few hundred people. I've attended these sorts of events many times, and I decided to "look for the money." I saw a table dominated by older, well-dressed folks, and I decided that was where I would settle in.

They were almost finished their shrimp cocktail appetizer; I apologized for my tardiness and offered to buy wine for the table. The wine arrived and was poured, but as I went to lay my wine menu down on the table, it bumped a glass of red wine onto the lap of the gentleman next to me. I was horrified! I apologized profusely and servers rushed to his aid with many white linen napkins. Others at the table tried to calm us down and began asking about where I had travelled from and what my specific company did. I was well into describing my environmental consulting work, when a puzzled young man at the table asked, "You know you are at the Chartered Professional Accountants of Nova Scotia annual meeting, right?"

I didn't know that, nor did I know that the gentleman I had spilt wine on was the keynote speaker for the evening. All I remember after that was him asking me for my business card and me slinking quickly from the room. Oddly, the meeting I was supposed to attend was being held through another door a few feet from the first door I had entered… I don't remember, or perhaps I chose to block everything out, after that.

That was an excellent opportunity for me to observe shallow, ego-driven interests over the benefit of using conferences and meetings to engage in authentic dialogue and relationship building. I was thoroughly embarrassed by my attendance at the Chartered Professional Accountants meeting, but it did allow me the opportunity to entertain my colleagues with the story on many subsequent occasions. Self-deprecation can be a helpful tool to make others feel more comfortable.

Most professionals prefer not to "sell" their expertise (at least not as I was trying to in Halifax). They want to be hired for their known skills and experience and for their ability to credibly address and resolve technical issues and approvals. "Selling" their company or themselves seems to cheapen their impression of their value and importance in the marketplace. They believe that they should simply need to complete sound technical work and gain repeat business from existing clients. That's an important part of every successful consulting practice, but there is a fundamental component that will more effectively allow you to out-position your competitors. Knowledge sharing (without attaching costs) opens the door to genuine relationship development and long-term client–consultant affiliations.

Most clients are much more interested in learning information that will assist them in maintaining and growing their own operations. Clients, potential clients, regulators, and new team members would prefer to be attracted to your firm because they sense you are able to provide

- awareness of legislation, policy, and technical trends/issues affecting them;
- guidance regarding the intersection of environmental, social, and economic fields of inquiry;
- awareness of modernized and/or innovative approaches that are working more effectively in various jurisdictions; and
- guidance regarding how they might begin to think differently about their own desired outcomes.

Positioning yourself and your firm as knowledgeable, approachable experts who are useful to interact with is far more effective than having the best candies at your tradeshow booth.

Finding the work means finding the clients and projects that will fit with your interests and collective skills. It's also important to have a clear understanding of the services you provide strength in, as you assess your fit with potential clients. Figure 2 provides a consolidated services list for environmental consultants, the market I know best. It is broad and not intended to be all inclusive, but it may be helpful to glance at to see how diverse the services are that your firm offers. It also provides an example of how services might be better organized and understood.

TYPES OF CONSULTANTS

1. **Greenfield and Blue Water Environments** *existing, natural* **(relatively undeveloped lands and waters)** *landscapes*
   - Terrain/Landscape Evaluation
   - Hydrological Sciences (marine and freshwater)
   - Hydrogeological Sciences
   - Lake Capacity
   - Marine Ecology
   - Coastal Zone Planning and Management
   - Air Quality
   - Ecosystem Planning and Management
   - Environmental Impact Assessment (broadly speaking should include social, cultural, economic, and balanced outcomes)
   - Permitting and Monitoring
   - Ecological Restoration/Rewilding *Kids might understand*
   - Mitigation Planning, Monitoring, and Management (including *easier* mitigation banking)
   - Natural Resources Management

the terminology we use with the audience is important

2. Contaminated Land and Water Environments/ Effluent Testing (relatively developed/impacted lands and waters)

- Environmental Health and Safety Management and Compliance
- Contamination Assessment and Remediation
- Risk Management
- Ecotoxicology
- Toxicity Testing
- Compliance and Due Diligence
- Health-based Risk Assessments
- Site Remediation
- Noise and Vibration Management
- Emergency and Spill Response
- Environmental Management Systems

3. Policy/Regulatory Approaches

- Strategic and Regulatory Planning   *Environmental planner*
- Program Evaluation
- Regulatory and Policy Reform
- Analyses of Proposed Legislation and Regulation
- Public–Private Partnerships

4. Emerging/Innovative Services

- eDNA
- Remote Sensing Advances and Strategies *, drones*
- Sustainability Strategies and Sustainable Development
- Climate Resiliency and Adaptation
- Smarter Impact Assessment*, go baseline conditions*
- Strategic Advisory Services (more complete integration of ecological, social, cultural, and economic considerations in impact assessment)

- diversity, social, landscape → -more socio-economic cultural

- measuring biodiversity w/ acoustic monitoring
- using wifi signal to bounce of bodies & count them.

↑ AIA is not on this idea yet ↳ international impact assessment association.

Figure 2: Consolidated Service List for Environmental Consultants

The traditional, aggressive, and largely unenlightened approach to sales is still far too common. It's normal to find conventional and typical websites, tradeshow spaces, and even social media flooded with unaware, self-serving, or unconscious messages (e.g., lengthy lists of services and projects, overt self-interested campaigns to lure clients). Far less common are examples of transformative approaches that focus on the conveyance of knowledge and information that will help the client base achieve their objectives more effectively. Out-dated approaches that linger and remain common in books, events, and training sessions are those that are unrelated to the sharing of important interpretations, understandings, trends, and strategic advantages of new thinking and approaches.

As the environmental consulting industry continues to grow and change, a critical ingredient in successful sales is an ability to think differently and find more innovative processes and outcomes.

Conferences and Tradeshows

In a simple example of a sales approach, consider the typical 8'×10' tradeshow booth. After a few hours at a large event, the booths begin to blend together: piles of business cards, lists of services, and odd samples and pieces of equipment on display, for example, can cause a numbing of the brain. If the tradeshow is worth the marketing investment, it's worth thinking differently and strategically about how best to deliver the results and separate your firm from the dozens of similar groups.

One experience that stands out for me was a tradeshow that Savanta took seriously and planned strategically for in 2018. We invested time developing a differentiating approach that gained significant positive feedback from attendees. Rather than customary and common approaches, we decided to upend tradition and professionally designed a booth that promoted genuine engagement. We were able to work with a talented design firm Field Trip & Co, in Toronto to create an impactful and interactive display. The following are a few design sketches that helped guide the creation of the tradeshow booth.

We adopted an approach of giving back to, rather than taking from, the attendees. We adopted a humble and helpful attitude, rather than a self-interested, egoic, me-first sales approach. We carefully considered what the participants would appreciate learning about, and it wasn't a list of our services. We selected a booth design that provided useful information about the automation of field-data collection and how one endangered species has recovered well in the United States (Michigan in particular) and seems to be gaining a more significant foothold in Canada. We didn't have to tell clients and competitors that we are specialists in endangered species or that we were the creators of an innovative ecological fieldwork app; they figured that out on their own.

We won the best-booth award at the show, which was attended by some 600 individuals involved in the conservation movement and environmental industry in Ontario. Our success in that conference and trade-show was increased by our strategic and intensive approach to ensuring we were able to present several helpful and informative technical papers.

Our approach also inspired the Savanta team members in attendance. These words are from one of our team members (addressing our entire company):

> Hi everyone—just thought I'd share the good word that Savanta was quite successful at this year's conference. As you know we had two adjacent booths to showcase the functionality of our app and the work that's been done with the Kirtland's warbler project. ... Our team members did an exceptional job presenting their work to date and spreading interest in a globally imperilled species. I had multiple people tell me how blown away they were by the magnitude of this project and its progression... At the end of it all, attendees were asked to vote on their favourite booths based on three categories. Savanta

cleaned up here, winning two of the three awards (Best looking exhibit space and Best staff discussion).

… Our team members at the booth showed extrasensory perception like I've never seen before. When an interested guest would approach the booth, they'd jointly promote the app, seamlessly throwing out helpful information back and forth, as if they'd rehearsed for hours beforehand. They were like Olympian synchronized swimmers.

While they were not Olympic synchronized swimmers, they were ecologists who were (and are) passionate about the work they do—and it showed. It's that type of feedback that helps highlight the importance of thinking differently and treating clients, potential clients, and colleagues with transparency, kindness, and respect. If you are involved in any trade-show or conference event, it's time to open your mind to new approaches that can lead to genuine engagement and differentiation. Focus less on me-first self-promotion and more on how to generate value for all attendees—that's the nature of the needed transformation. And that means being self-aware and understanding the role of your ego in marketing.

Similar things can be said about other important aspects of direct marketing (e.g., market research, lead development, networking, proposals, presentations) and indirect marketing (e.g., publications, advertising, websites, social media, becoming a visible expert, awards programs, giving back). Specific to the following topics below, I offer a few comments about some of the more important lessons I have learned. They also provide an illustration of how to transform opportunities into differentiating actions.

Websites

Again, this area of marketing needs transformation. Differentiation and uniqueness are important. How do you create website content that is useful and informative versus content that is simply self-serving? Websites can be powerful tools when designed and maintained with intention. Websites that are just static and stale sales vehicles with typical and routine content headings (e.g., Services, Markets, Expertise, People, Projects, Locations) are being replaced by more meaningful and creative content.

Stepping back and rethinking your brand and associated messaging can take some time and investment, but firms that want to be part of the leading edge of a transforming consulting industry and retain the best staff and clients will wisely choose to make those investments. The following extract from Pinsky's (2018) article, "Eleven Design and Development Best Practices for 2018," resonates with me:

> To capitalize on opportunity and captivate real, live, human readers, an optimized, functional, interactive website is a must. Unfortunately, the Internet is swarming with poor website designs that miss both the technical and content mark. Worse yet, clients and developers alike continuously contribute to the current outbreak of design delinquency in equal measure.... Clients believe that as long as their site "looks good", it will float in cyberspace, effectively extending brand reach while magically attracting millions of interested users and converting them into customers.... The truth is that's not how website magic works. To deliver digital results, a website must offer an engaging, dynamic user experience.

There is lots of information online about how to design and build websites and what trends are emerging in the design industry. It's worth engaging a skilled design firm to support your initiative, unless of course you are fluent in and adept at considering topics such as design communications, branding, mobile-friendly design, progressive web apps, machine learning and artificial intelligence, dark mode, and intentional imperfections.

Social Media

I have personally found that LinkedIn is a preferred social media and business platform that can support and help develop a consulting firm's (and individual staff's) reach. I have tinkered with Instagram, Twitter, and Facebook and looked at other emerging platforms, but LinkedIn is the most useful for strategic business positioning. LinkedIn's vision is to *"create economic opportunity for every member of the global workforce."* Its mission is to *"connect the world's professionals to make them more productive and successful."*

Advice for LinkedIn users:

- Keep your profile current and share and post information that can contribute positively to the business audience.

- While LinkedIn discourages you from connecting with people you don't know, I suggest that you consider that advice with a grain of salt. LinkedIn is the world's largest business network, with more than 750 million users across 200 countries. It's well built for networking. Understandably, it's the ignorant and disrespectful use that I imagine LinkedIn is trying to control with its suggestion to connect only with people that you know. Respect and honour all individuals that you interact with.

- Shift away from the hard-core, me-first sales approaches. Rather, move towards providing valuable and useful content without aggressively positioning for subscriber fees or emails to feed alternative revenue streams.

- Be respectful and positive. Thank people who accept your invitation to connect. It's not an Easter egg or Pokémon hunt, where you are after as many connections as you can grab without attention to relevance or grace. LinkedIn opens doors to establish new and decent professional relationships.

- Engage mindfully, reflecting an understanding of the different culture and language of the connection. Use your connections' native language, if you can, as a sign of respect. (*Google Translate* seems to be helpful in this regard).

There is also much information about the importance and relevance of blogs, networking, pro bono work, position papers, speaking, and testimonials, some of which might be helpful and appropriate for your consultancy (Weiss 2011). Again, the most successful approaches will be those that are not egoic and that share thoughtful and useful information. Free, shared content is the new normal in many business sectors.

Proposals and Presentations

Proposals

Different markets and clients require and often expect different proposal formats. Where a well-written Terms of Reference is available, make sure you invest enough time to completely understand that document and ensure that you provide all required information. You don't want to lose out or be downgraded because of a simple omission.

Gartner (2008) identifies and expands upon seven characteristics that help to generate winning proposals. They are

- clarity;
- responsive;
- people-oriented;
- brevity;
- hot buttons;
- theme; and
- organization.

These characteristics are fairly standard aspects that all bidders should consider. Personally, I would add innovative to that list.

When bidding on private-sector work in particular, I have used various delivery styles and approaches for differentiation purposes and to excite the potential client about our bid. These tactics have included

- magazine-style formats;
- video and audio tracks of the site(s) and interviews with stakeholders; and
- translation, where appropriate, into the language of parent companies and company representatives.

On one project, the environmental approvals for a new golf-resort development, we developed a movie tour of the ecological features and functions in which the golf course layout would sit. That video allowed the developers and their investors to virtually visit the lands and waters as part of visioning the origins and outcome of the development.

One of the strangest proposals that I have been involved with was in Cartagena, Colombia. I was sent to Cartagena to meet with a local firm that wanted to partner with us on a coastal-zone plan and clean-up. A local guide escorted me in his small motorboat to get a sense of the discharge outlets polluting the bay. During about 30 minutes of travel, I took pictures of industrial outfalls into the sea, using a telephoto lens.

To my great surprise, a military gunboat rolled up beside us and ordered us to a nearby dock. I sat in the boat under an armed guard while my guide was whisked away in a military truck. I knew no Spanish, and I wondered how the event would end. After what seemed like hours (I think it was only 30 minutes), my guide was returned to the boat. We quickly left the dock, and the guide told me that the military was concerned that I was a terrorist plotting to blow up one of their industrial facilities. Submitting a proposal was not looking encouraging.

I returned to my hotel to find it bursting with people… and motorbikes. I quickly learned that my trip to Cartagena coincided with a large regional Harley Davidson biker festival. The city was swarming with thousands of bikers from all over Central and South America. That night my hotel caught fire.

I was grateful to make it to the airport the next morning for my flight back to Canada. Unfortunately, the pilot announced as he was taxiing to the runway that an instrument light had come on, and we were returning to the terminal. We waited for 13 hours in the departure lounge—a room without a washroom. Every time a passenger had to go to the washroom, they were frisked to get back into the departure lounge. It was a disturbing period, and I lost track of how many security hands were groping and grabbing at my body.

Finally, close to midnight, amidst a chorus of cheers, the airline shuttled us to a hotel overnight. Fortunately, that hotel did not catch fire. I safely returned to Canada the next day. The chaos and risks encountered and the local partner's insistence that he be allocated ten percent of the project budget for "administration" costs caused me to decline to bid.

Presentations

Presentations aren't scary when you are comfortable with and believe in the content that you are delivering. I have had the privilege of presenting before small audiences of a dozen people to hundreds of attendees at conferences in overflowing ballrooms. I've enjoyed the smaller gatherings more because it feels easier to make connections with audience members and participants.

I take the same approach to presentations that I do in my personal and professional life. I'm interested in sharing only the best ideas I can muster without worrying about attracting business. It's like billable time in a consulting company: if you guide and inspire team members to love what they do, increased utilization levels will result. Browbeating and embarrassing people because they didn't hit billing targets often has the opposite effects (e.g., guilt, shame, frustration, resentment).

Enter into any presentation with a positive attitude. Be fully present when you are on stage at the podium. Be authentic and do your best to share your knowledge and wisdom. Focus on engaging with people who seem interested in understanding your ideas. Don't pursue presentations with the notion that you have to generate a business card collection and close sales. Be helpful, curious, and generous in how you communicate. When you do that, you will naturally attract similarly authentic people and relationships.

Ensure that you are well prepared to share your thoughts. Plan carefully, rehearse the timing, and as you begin to speak, tell people what you will say, say it, and then tell them what you just told them. Use compelling and simple graphics and slides. Don't cram all of your information into a slide deck, hoping that the audience will somehow read every word. Present information, as clearly as you can, using no more than one slide for every minute of your timeslot. And remember to thank the audience and host for the opportunity to share your thoughts with them.

One of my more difficult speeches was given when I was in the United Arab Emirates for an environmental conference. I had gotten food poisoning from eating at a restaurant the night before my talk, and as I stood at the podium giving my speech, I was trembling and sweating. Somehow I made it through my presentation (a summary of environmental technologies in Canada) and headed straight back to the Armed Forces Officers Club, my hotel in Abu Dhabi. For a few days I was there in bed regaining my strength and booking and rebooking my return trip each day. The housekeeping staff were not amused. I learned not to eat sour cream in the desert.

Key Points and Observations in Chapter 4:

Finding the Work –
A Shifting Approach to Marketing and Sales

1. We are in a transformative period in the marketing and sales aspects of consulting. It's not important to tell clients how wonderful you are or to give them a long list of services that you can provide. And it's not appropriate to try to lure and outsmart clients. That's your and your company's collective egos talking. It's time to observe and manage our egos far more effectively and to neutralize and abandon the hard-core, me-first sales approach.

2. At events, focus less on self-promotion and more on how to generate value for all attendees—that's the nature of the needed transformation. And that means being self-aware and understanding the role of your ego in marketing.

3. Adopt an approach of giving back to, not taking from, your network. Adopt a humble and helpful attitude rather than a self-interested, egoic, me-first sales approach.

4. Most clients are much more interested in learning information that will assist them in maintaining and growing their own operations. Position yourself and your firm as knowledgeable, approachable experts who are useful to interact with.

5. Websites can be powerful tools when designed and maintained with intention. Websites that are just static and stale sales vehicles with typical and routine content headings are beginning to be replaced by more meaningful and more creative content.

6. Don't eat sour cream in the desert.

Chapter 5

Managing and Delivering High-Quality, Credible Work

Doing the Work

THE TECHNICAL ASPECTS OF PROJECT MANAGEMENT ARE LOGICAL AND comprehensible and not that complicated (Gartner 2008). Good project management requires common sense, patience, discretion, self-discipline, people skills, and, above all, the proper attitude. Gartner describes that attitude as one of professionalism, where a project manager takes responsibility for every aspect of the project and focuses on the project's success.

Consultants bring a diverse skill set to the firm and their work, including different styles of written communication. Some are quite comfortable and adept at report development; others are less so. It's also been my observation that technical experts, while masters in their fields, tend not to be well trained in writing and sharing technical information in the clearest and most effective manner possible.

I was fortunate, early in my career, to have been mentored by John F. Gartner, the co-founder of Gartner Lee Limited in Ontario, Canada. John taught me quite a bit about marketing, strategic thinking, and writing. He gave me the opportunity to co-develop and co-implement an internal writing course at Gartner Lee. He influenced me to significantly improve my writing and my communications more generally.

In consulting, each of us has developed our own writing style and approach, typically through cumulative post-academic experience. That poses a challenge in the working world, where our individual and collective successes depend upon clear, consistent, and precise communications. It's important that our writing is easily understood by the target audiences. Written materials need to be honest, objective, and inclusive.

I love the use of the right words to convey effective messaging. Just ask any team member who has worked with me. Some will no doubt suggest that I needlessly offer minor edits to and comments on their reports and communications. Others will share that they are appreciative of the review processes and have benefitted in terms of their own writing skills. I do what I do because I love communicating with precision and with impact.

Gartner's (2008) book provides some excellent guidance to consultants wanting to write more effectively. A summary of some of his advice follows. John points out that instead of formulating the written plan, many people write while they are thinking about what to compose. A few of my favourite suggestions that he makes are as follows:

- write as you talk;
- keep sentences short, with one idea per sentence;
- be concise and mindful of the economy of words;
- limit the use of adjectives and avoid pompousness; and
- use active verbs.

Doing the work in consulting can sometimes be more difficult than it sounds. A project can have many facets, some of which can be complex. If you started the bid or the project with a clear understanding of the scope, objectives, and expected outcomes, then surprises should be limited.

If your firm is satisfied with average products and reporting, then you may choose not to control and manage the quality of your work. However, if you want your work to be well regarded and to stand up to client and regulatory scrutiny, then it's important to ensure that you and your firm have a clear and effective excellence assurance/excellence empowerment approach. Some people might prefer more traditional quality assurance/quality control tools and processes.

Although it should be considered typical and not transformative, I have often found the quality and readability of many consultant deliverables to be lacking, and in many cases, significantly so. Meaning, there is a need for an improved central technical and communications review function on all deliverables. Key aspects include:

- assigning technical review to the most experienced specialists in your firm;

- having someone or a team with excellent writing skills review deliverables for clarity and grammatical and spelling precision; and

- having a production department that is creative, innovative, responsive, and reliable.

Getting Paid for Your Work

In some standard operational areas of consulting, there are perhaps fewer opportunities for radical and helpful transformation. There are, however, many opportunities to ensure that at least best practices are improved and consistently applied.

As much as most consultants may not like dealing with financial and contractual matters, they are key to a company's success. Red flags to consultants should include a client's reluctance to sign an authorization or to provide a deposit or mobilization payment to initiate work. The beginning of a consulting assignment is the beginning of a new or continuing relationship with a client. Successfully initiating an agreement that allows work to begin is an opportunity to celebrate an exciting new initiative. It should be entered into with a clear understanding of scope, price, and terms of payment.

Unless you want your firm to depend more heavily on external financing (with associated borrowing costs), payment of your invoices in a timely manner is essential. To accomplish this, an ongoing and positive dialogue with clients is key. It's also important to remember that your employer is paying you for work that you completed and billed to the client long before those funds from the client are collected.

In many situations I have entered arrangements with known clients to move forward without formal contracts and procedures. In very few cases have I started working with new clients without some form of binding authorization. The type and nature of agreements vary; what's important is a common understanding of the work to be undertaken and how it will be completed. These processes can be simpler and less onerous in smaller consulting firms, although there may be some exposure to risk that is not fully contemplated by smaller firms without internal or readily accessible external legal expertise.

Larger firms and big, complex projects can include the requirement for more comprehensive and formal agreements. In some more litigious societies (e.g., the United States), formal agreements are necessary. I have included one of the now-dated standard terms and conditions documents that we used early on at Savanta (see the Appendix). This document was an effort to avoid complex, legalese language and lengthy agreements, while still trying to cover key principles and risks. This agreement was readily accepted by our clients, and litigation was never required to address any disagreements.

In fact, I have experienced only one lawsuit in my 40-year career, a lawsuit that I could only describe as frivolous and based on fiction. It's a claim by a client that our brief, one-day, off-season (late fall) field visit to lands they chose to buy should have been able to identify an endangered plant species that is visible only in the summer growing season. I expect that matter will be resolved, but I have learned to be prepared for anything in consulting, regardless of legitimacy.

One aspect of that litigation I found interesting was an opposing lawyer's attempts to bully me. Because of COVID-19, the proceedings were carried out on a Zoom call. The opposing lawyer chose to impose himself over and close to his camera as if he were trying to press his weight on me remotely. That egoic technique did not work, although I did find his approach amusing.

How long should you wait to get paid? Most consultants require payment thirty days from receipt of the invoice. Some sectors are slower to pay than others. In my experience, the public sector can be quite slow to process and pay consulting invoices. So can certain industry sectors (e.g., land development). I have learned through experience that some land developers have policies that they will not pay any consulting invoices before they age for 90 or more days. It's part of a tradition with some firms (even larger firms) where they unfairly rely, in part, on their suppliers to bankroll their projects.

And should you charge interest? Yes, it should be charged and collected; there is no reason for clients to hold on to your financial resources. You are actively paying salaries, taxes, benefits, and other suppliers on a regular basis (or at least you should be). Clients who do not respect these rules are better working with one of your competitors.

When do you seek various legal measures? Remember that business is about trying to maintain a respectful relationship with clients. If you are managing projects properly, you should be able to address and resolve any growing scope and associated charges on a regular basis. If you have not been treating a client respectfully in terms of billings, then you may need to deepen and intensify your dialogue with them.

If a client persists with excuses such as those that follow, try to address them. If they have been addressed and you feel as though you are getting the run-around, consider a discounted amount contingent on immediate payment or litigation as a last-ditch effort (e.g., in my Canadian province, Ontario, it may be through the Small Claims Court). In either case, quickly close the file or project, and when payment is received, send all relevant materials to the client to enable them to retain a new consulting firm that is willing to share and accept their values and approach to payment.

Examples of client responses you might receive:

- I haven't seen these invoices before.
- You need to change some particulars on the invoices (e.g., client name, subsidiary, address) before they can be processed.
- You have already billed to our agreed-upon budget; what is this invoice for?

Last resorts, which can include litigation, should rarely be needed. It's too late to be chasing funds through litigation, when you consider the potential impacts on your firm's costs and reputation, not to mention the time-consuming distraction that litigation can present. Keep a Deny List (not a blacklist, with its racist undertones) of unenlightened firms that everyone in your company knows are not desired as clients.

Work with clients who respect you, pay you, and share your values.

Finding the Next Job

Assuming you are producing solid work and achieving excellence with all of your deliverables, you will receive new work by reputation. That may not be enough if you are in a highly competitive industry or geography, or if you are investing in efforts to grow your firm.

One area where transformative opportunities exist is with client relationships. We need to adopt a new way of thinking. We are adept at ego-driven relationships that depend upon selling our reasons why a client should want to hire us again. I have noticed that men are particularly adroit at superficial, ego-driven, sales-oriented relationships.

As consultants, we are generally less skilled at fostering a genuine relationship with clients that will leave the door open for honest and direct dialogue about how we can continue to provide professional services that are insightful and useful. Schein (2016) refers to the need for a new attitude of humility in our relationships with clients. Schein notes: *"I am there to help work things out together, not to take over the problem and run with it. I am there to empathetically honor the difficulties the client faces."*

According to Balardo (2019): *"We are guests in the client's house and need to behave accordingly."* He also says: *"It's all about the client. You want to do your best to make them successful while not seeking glory."* These are the ideas and approaches that can allow us to create and sustain client relationships with a well-managed role for our egos.

Depending upon existing client relationships for repeat business can take some of the pressure off the finding new clients. Traditionally, businesses would target sixty percent to eighty percent repeat business with existing clients (Gartner 2008). That percentage may still be reasonable to ensure consistent revenue flows, but the client base is changing rapidly (through business failures, mergers, acquisitions), and more effort will be needed to maintain existing relationships and to seek out new clients.

Weiss (2011) defines repeat business according to the following four types:

- More work for the same buyer of the same kind;
- More work for the same buyer of a different kind;
- Work for other buyers within the same client of the same kind; and
- Work for other buyers within the same client of a different kind.

The rapidly changing client base will place increasing pressure on some firms with high fixed costs. It will also favour those that operate remotely with less dependence upon brick and mortar office facilities and those who are able to move more quickly and nimbly in the market (e.g., niche or boutique companies).

Managing, Sculpting, and Evolving a Business

Depending upon your role in your consulting firm, you may be more involved in the operation of the overall business. The manager's role in an operation depends upon the type, scale, and goals of a company.

Managing a business requires a particular focus on generating revenues, managing projects and handling costs and other strategic investments. An annual budget (and plan) is essential to be able to guide the progress of a firm over time. As you deal with your projects, clients, and business, the following are some highlights to be considered related to managing costs, revenues, debt, and equity.

Costs are usually described as being direct (e.g., salary) or indirect (e.g., marketing, education, research). Salary costs are the largest fixed cost (although they are really an investment) in a consulting firm. If you position your firm to have the best capabilities, you will be able to command higher billing rates, and you will be able to pay higher than average salaries to attract and keep the best talent. Having the best people will also significantly increase the value of intangibles in your firm (e.g., staff loyalty, judgement, and commitment; synergies; innovations; enthusiasm).

An opportunity now exists to begin to transform how accounting and legal aspects of a firm are addressed. I know that internal corporate accountants and controllers prefer to tightly regulate costs as a general approach to doing their jobs. That work is vital to the health of an organization, but taking it too seriously, with an overly aggressive approach, can lead to unintended consequences. Those consequences can include demotivating staff, missing opportunities, and declining to engage in strategic initiatives (e.g., enhanced IT hardware and software, custom app development, thoughtful and meaningful research).

An overly risk-averse legal approach can similarly negatively affect a firm's credibility and standing with clients, team members, and various stakeholders. Decisions at a corporate level need to be made with egos and self-interest set aside. Doing so will help shift away from control to genuine accountability.

Operational transformation will benefit from empowering consultants to be fully responsible for client engagement and project profitability and reminding operational staff that they are there to provide two types of support: (1) general corporate support and (2) specific, positive support to the individual consultants and their teams (i.e., the consultants aren't there to service operational staff).

I heard of one interaction amongst operational and technical staff that surprised me (and it takes a lot to surprise me anymore). The billing specialist was called by another administrative team member to discuss an invoicing matter. The billing specialist immediately started swearing and belittling project managers as idiots who didn't know crap about what they were doing. The technical project manager, who was sitting quietly on the call waiting to speak, was then introduced. Awkwardness pervaded the rest of the call, and the verbally abusive billing specialist immediately offered that her complaint wasn't directed to the technical project manager on the call. Without authenticity, individuals in consulting can abruptly stumble.

There can sometimes be a challenging dynamic between the consulting and operational sides of business, especially when it comes to innovation and transformation. A leader who can step away from egoic positions and make timely decisions that will improve outcomes, will advance a company's shift towards enlightenment. From a leader's perspective, doing what's right won't always be doing what is most convenient or what is least likely to generate dissent.

In senior management, leaders need to be able to make decisions without undue reliance on advice from a handful of like-minded individuals. A leader's strength of character will truly advance a firm and its team's interests, while setting the tone and culture of the firm and while depending upon a skilled team of operations and administrative staff that service and support the firm's individual consultants.

Costs that don't need to occur in a consulting company are those associated with write-offs and inappropriate proposal investments. My experience has suggested the biggest contributors to those issues are

- lacklustre project and client management;
- clients who use non-payment as a method of managing their own costs; and
- thoughtless and irresponsible proposal chasing.

When we don't communicate regularly with clients about budgets and scope changes, we risk falling offside. Not wanting to irritate or nickel and dime clients needs to be balanced with effective and timely communications and accurate budget tracking. While avoiding write-offs, we also need to be honest and transparent with staff. Some team members might be pouring time into projects to demonstrate that they can meet their utilization targets, hoping somehow that clients will happily pay for the excesses. This practice is inappropriate and should be promptly addressed.

We also need to be open, truthful, and transparent with our clients. I have worked with some who seem reluctant to pay their invoices—and not because they don't appreciate the work or because the scope has changed. Some clients prefer to hold onto their cash for at least 90 days after receipt of invoices, effectively using their consultants to financially support their projects. These are relationships that are unrewarding and will lead to increased business costs (i.e., continuing to borrow and pay interest on your line of credit). Some staff may experience a general malaise towards servicing those clients. I suggest you release those clients and leave them to your competitors.

Thoughtless, scattered, and reactive proposal chasing is a challenging activity in consulting. There are many go–no go decision-making tools that help to define the questions we need to ask ourselves when deciding whether to bid. Committing to a bid on a public-sector proposal can be especially costly, so decisions on these bids, in particular need to be thoroughly considered. They can require staged submissions and multiple interviews and can be heavily weighted towards selecting the lowest-priced submission.

Consider the following questions as you apply a more thoughtful decision-making approach regarding whether to bid on a request for proposal:

- Why are we interested in bidding on this assignment (e.g., egoic and status interests, aligns with our values/corporate strategy, desperate for billable work)?

- Will our role on this assignment help create better and more meaningful outcomes for the client (why and how)?

- Do we have time to prepare a thorough, thoughtful, and high-quality submission?

- Do we have the right team to bid, given our internal and external networks, and given what we know about how well our team will match the client team?

- Have we been following this bid for some time, and have we accumulated information and advice that will help us successfully compete, or has this request come out of the blue?

Reflect carefully on these questions and design your own go–no go decision-making tool that fits with your own enterprise.

I'd suggest investing more time developing and implementing proposal decisioning in a more discerning manner than investing time and money in typical and traditional sales-training bootcamps and courses. Make sure that a decision to bid isn't grounded in an ego's desire to be seen as the author of an outcome (e.g., project recognition, awards) or to futilely fight against a decline in business. New work doesn't flow smoothly to people whose egos get in the way. And the days of depending upon friends in the industry handing you work are dwindling.

Invest in helping consultants develop their self-awareness. Unless there are compelling reasons to bid, you may be better off devoting some of that proposal response time to more strategic and forward-thinking initiatives—initiatives that will truly differentiate your firm.

In terms of managing a business, a few other topics are worth considering. For example, how do you decide your billing rates and utilization targets (something that relates to your financial model)? This is a large topic that is covered in depth by other authors (e.g., Gartner 2008). I offer a few observations that point to the need to clearly understand where your firm is currently positioned on the price and value index, and where you want it to be positioned. This and other topics (e.g., managing costs and revenues, shareholding, profit sharing) are further discussed in the following pages.

Over the past four decades, I have observed and participated in many corporate financial models. In some cases, significant units with firms (e.g., remediation, geotechnical, soils, archaeology) decided that they were in very price-sensitive markets and that their billing rates needed to be lower than others in the firm (in some cases negatively affecting a firm's ability to meet revenue and profitability targets). Discussions about whether to remain in these markets or how to evolve in these markets to offer and bill for the provision of more value are rarely fully transparent, honest, and complete.

It's okay to create a firm that operates in a price-sensitive market. Many aspects of traditional consulting that once achieved higher levels of profitability are becoming commoditized, so much so that low bids and marginal profit margins are the results. When engaging in those markets, don't plan to become an innovative firm; simply accept and embrace the fact that you are destined to have certain limits on your firm's growth, meaningful impacts, and profitability.

We would all benefit from discussions that are more transparent, but also discussions that are based upon collaboration and not grounded in egoic thinking. Ensure you are collaborating with people who are on track and moving toward a position of self-awareness. Avoid allowing your (or others') ego to hijack reasonable and open dialogue. Leave your ego at the door when you sit down with your team to discuss what markets make sense to engage in. Then you will truly be sculpting the character of a successful firm.

A firm needs to carefully think through its current and desired position in the market. Considerations to establishing fair and reasonable billing rates include the following:

- Is your firm staffed with the best experts in the industry?
- Are some of your experts thought leaders?
- Will the client base support higher billing rates in exchange for streamlined approvals, reduced timeframes, and other innovations?
- Does the client base want better outcomes, or are they simply looking for straightforward solutions at the lowest price?

Should a firm have multiple billing rates for individuals in different markets? I have participated in models with standard billing rates that are reduced only for self-designed research aspects of projects. I have also participated in models with multiple billing rate tables used for the same staff with different clients (e.g., public versus private). It's a matter of perspective. If your billing rate reasonably reflects a mark-up on an individual's salary, why would you want to discount a rate without discounting the respective salary? That's a simple question to consider that requires transparency and dialogue within and external to your firm.

You may decide in some circumstances to reduce a bid as a strategic move to access a specific project or market but developing and applying different rate tables for different markets can feel and be disingenuous and manipulative.

When it comes to setting prices for work (e.g., scope of services, proposals), explore other options, including, for example, the use of a final proposal price discount, fixed-fee or lump-sum billing, and value billing.

Fixed-fee or lump-sum billing allows you to bid a fixed, final price, and to deliver the intended outcome(s) as efficiently as you can—which could mean increased profit margins. It could also mean substantially reduced profit margins if you encounter unexpected delays or costs that cannot be addressed through reasonable scope changes.

Value billing is a term encountered more often at the senior levels of an organization, where a person decides they will charge more for their services than the time they spent on a file to inflate the profit margins on those assignments. These individuals claim that their time is worth more than the hours billed. I am not in favour of this type of inauthentic billing. Others seem to find it sits well with them.

Public-sector work typically costs more to acquire, often through pre-qualifications processes, proposals, presentations, and contract negotiations. And in some cases, work can be billed only at designated milestones and be subject to holdbacks until the successful completion of the entire assignment. Designing your billing system to record as little as ten- or fifteen-minute increments can help increase accountability and can contribute to more accurate billing. It should, however, be understood that public bids will erode the profitability of your firm.

Typically, private-sector work is more relationship-based and may or may not include competitive bids. Recognizing these differences is important to making strategic decisions regarding where you and your firm want to complete most of your work. The public sector can have many interesting and innovative opportunities and can include larger scales of assignments. I have found a 70:30 or 80:20 mix of private to public work tends to include enough market diversity, stability, and security, while still optimizing revenues, profits, and the ability to give back.

In terms of ongoing operations and growth, consulting companies rely upon a variety of sources of capital (e.g., banks, share issuance, shareholder loans, venture capital). Business planning needs to demonstrate the predicted flow of revenues and profits to engage and interest investors and share purchasers. I have chosen to invest in small and larger firms' shares only when I have had an opportunity to fully understand several important considerations:

- Is the share valuation based upon standard and accepted accounting practices? (This requires and benefits from third-party accounting and legal advice.)
- Is there transparency around the share types, structure, and individual allocations?
- Are there clear and transparent rules available around how profits and dividends are distributed?
- Is the company business and succession planning clear and available for review and consideration?

- Are the terms around the internal and external sale of shares clear and transparent?

In my experience, shareholding is not a preferred financial investment compared with other more typical market investments (i.e., in normal markets, if they exist post–COVID-19). But, if you believe that you are in the right firm, you want a voice at the decision-making table, and you are there for the long term, it may make sense to acquire shares. The acquisition of shares should provide you with a clearly defined career path, projections of share-value growth and dividend/bonus distribution, and an understanding of how the share value will be protected over time against major disruptive changes in the financial and client markets.

The consultants who benefit the most from shareholding are generally the founders and most senior owners. Founders, who in most cases built the business from scratch, profit the most from internal and even more from external share sales. Lots of investor-related questions confront owners and managers over time:

- When do we invite new shareholders in (if not all staff are eligible for shares)?

- What percentage of staff should be owners? Gartner (2008), for example, suggests 10 percent.

- Can goodwill value be added in for internal share sales (e.g., client loyalty, market position, costs that are best described as strategic investments)?

- How will profits be distributed and to whom (e.g., just shareholders or all staff)?

- What percentage of profits should be distributed according to ownership versus merit bonuses to any contributing team member?

These questions require substantial discussions and the input of advice from experienced accounting and legal professionals. There are no simple answers to many of these questions. It's perhaps easier to begin to define the key principles that underlie your firm, some of which might include variations of the following:

- All team members are important; we will respect, manage, and reward all our team members for their work.

- We include innovation in our work, wherever possible, to generate better and more meaningful outcomes for our clients.

- Our company distributes profits on an annual basis, when and if profits are available.

- Sixty percent of profits go to investors and shareholders who have built and/or are continuing to fund the growth of the business.

- Forty percent of profits go to all staff who have helped grow and strengthen our firm.

- Opportunities for staff to purchase shares will be made periodically/annually and will be based upon known and shared criteria.

Ensuring you have a steady and consistent stream of revenue coming into a consulting firm is fundamental to success, even during challenging economic times. Unfortunately, many managers concentrate too much on cost reduction during difficult times, when attention needs to be equally or more focused on revenue generation. Innovative marketing approaches and strategic ideas to increase revenue flows are needed, especially to buffer against the effects of turbulent times.

Firms that are transforming their marketing approaches and thinking differently will outpace those who depend upon typically stale and cookie-cutter approaches. I have been fortunate to be able to continue to operate and to grow consulting firms even during the 2008–2009 "Great Recession" in Canada.

How a firm is led, how it operates, and how it communicates both internally and externally will help to define its character. The positives and the negatives experienced by a firm over time can affect its credibility and integrity and its place in the industry. A company's positive reputation depends upon honesty, transparency, active listening, and the delivery of consistent messaging. Depending upon the size of an organization, reputations can be negatively affected by individuals who are not in alignment with the firm on some of these important factors. Avoid aligning yourself with inauthentic and manipulative colleagues and leaders. Being truthful with staff and clients underpins successful relationships.

We are encountering a transformation across all businesses and platforms in response to the COVID-19 pandemic and in reaction to the citizens who are tired of and enraged by ongoing oppression and racism. An opportunity has been presented to all organizations, including consulting businesses, to carefully examine the biases of individuals and teams and to develop and implement a plan that will embrace diversity and foster activities and messages that will improve dialogue and outcomes. That means going beyond thinking and the formation of internal committees; it means acting boldly and progressively.

A diverse pool of consultants allows firms to allocate the right resources to activities and projects. It enables a firm to better match the style and approach of the client and engage the right skills for the right consulting team roles. These opportunities will be effective only if they are clearly and completely understood and don't just result in the sporadic appointment of individuals to serve as token representations of diversity. Teams need to reflect a more global character and include a diversity of perspectives across gender, race, belief systems, cultures, and age. They need to understand inclusivity and act more inclusively.

The inclusion of diversity and the opposition of racism and intolerance require taking the time to truly listen to and understand people. Inclusion also means connecting with people with a commitment to common decency. We have seen and are continuing to see a troubling shift towards a more common indecency, perpetuated by leaders who seem to believe that juvenile behaviours—such as name calling, belittling, and the use of fear—are appropriate management techniques. Accepting and living in apparent acceptance with those false beliefs will erode the credibility of individuals and firms. Instead of indecency, we need to shift the pendulum back towards decency, which can be described as the demonstration of courtesy, respect, and politeness; qualities that are expected in civilized societies.

The extreme perspectives of some leaders in political and civil society are resulting in misinformed and noisy proclamations related, at least in part, to ill-informed and illegitimate claims of rights (e.g., White supremacist messaging and actions). Because these actions seem to be confined to smaller, marginalized groups across political and economic spectra, one can hope that a larger, more genuine shift towards self-awareness can support the crafting and maintenance of consulting firms with an authentic and purposeful character.

For women in the consulting industry, do you feel respected and treated with equity in every aspect of your work? *Power Shift* (Armstrong 2019) speaks to allowing women and girls to walk alongside men and boys. The consulting industry, companies, and individuals will benefit significantly from the equitable inclusion of women at all levels.

Unfortunately, the consulting industry remains male dominated and so do the boardrooms, although that is slowly being corrected. Old boys' clubs are fading away, in some cases grudgingly, being replaced with a unified and equitable approach to leadership. Firms that understand this shift and actively participate in a more rapid and authentic leadership transformation, which is more equitable and inclusive, are those that will prosper.

Once a diverse team is assembled, integrated, and is functioning well, it's important to look at roles and responsibilities and career-path planning more carefully. It's unusual to find individuals who are skilled in every aspect of consulting. It's more typical to find some who like to sell their firm's services, some who like to manage projects and clients, and others who prefer to immerse themselves in the detailed technical work that serves as the foundation of projects and assignments.

Beyond where consulting staff seem to best fit in a broad functional role, it's vital to identify and develop roles and responsibilities collaboratively with consulting team members. Assumptions about roles and periodic reviews (e.g., once per year) are inadequate to build and sustain a successful practice.

Another aspect of the character of a firm is whether and how it gives back to the communities and citizens with which it is associated. Giving back is an expression of generosity and kindness, and while it shouldn't be done with an expectation of gaining benefits, giving programs and actions will contribute to the credibility and effectiveness of your consulting organization. Giving back is part of the character of the most successful consulting firms. It's also an opportunity for companies to connect team members with the communities in which they work. And it generally results in a more productive and engaged workforce. When a company is working on purpose and the team members are in alignment with that purpose, positive business outcomes are the natural result.

Different approaches exist to facilitate giving back. Some firms, for example, commit a percentage of revenues or profits to communities and causes that are important to them and their consulting team members. Other firms also grant their team members several paid days off a year to support them undertaking volunteer activities. These approaches allow the broader corporate team to feel a greater sense of purpose in their careers.

Several groups have been established to help companies give back. Giving Tuesday is a movement that harvests interest and investments following the consumer-saturated Black Friday and Cyber Monday shopping frenzies. Canada Helps promotes *"Giving made simple."* It helps to showcase charitable leaders and to coordinate donations.

Similar organizations exist throughout the world, including

- Giving USA;
- Charitable Giving UK and
- Charity Navigator.

Giving back will be more meaningful when it is connected to your company and team members in significant ways. Ask your team members and colleagues to help identify meaningful organizations that merit ongoing, not sporadic, contributions.

Consulting firms that have a strong altruistic character will see that character reflected in the value of the business, which brings to mind some ideas I'd like to offer about shares, valuation, ownership, and succession.

Bringing a Business to a Conclusion or the Next Chapter

There are a few common reasons to bring a company to a close or to begin a new chapter. You may

- need to liquidate the firm to access capital locked in the business;
- have partners who aren't interested in the leader's continuing role and the current value proposition;
- want to scale up the firm and your interests demand substantial capital that isn't easily accessible;
- have been approached by one or more firms who are interested in acquiring your business; and/or
- want to retire or change your professional focus.

There is nothing unusual about any of these and other reasons. What's more, it's about how to make the right decision and how to execute it to your and your team's advantage.

If you want to sell your firm, I will offer a couple of observations. Because internal sales rarely consider the value of goodwill, you will gain more money with an external sale to a larger firm with available cash than you will with an internal sale to current and new shareholders. As a firm's leader, recognize that you may face greater challenges holding your team together (and the associated value) before and after an external sale. So, the direction in terms of a sale depends in part upon the interests of the key owners and consideration of the legacy that leadership wants to leave behind, including the ongoing dynamic with team members.

Often, mounting pressure from within a firm can help to define the timing of a sale. If shareholding has not been offered to key professionals and they are growing concerned with their interpretation or understanding of the distribution of profits, it's time to consider options. In a well-run firm, you are already ahead of these types of issues and are not pushed into reactions. You may choose to take a long-term view and play a guiding role to new ownership and management that will pay out a reasonable price over a longer period. If money is not an overriding factor to the seller, that approach can work. There is increased uncertainty with the ability to see those longer-term payment plans properly implemented, and an external sale may eventually be required.

If, as the firm's leader, you are planning to stay on and work with the new or promoted internal management team, you will need to manage your ego and encourage, not discourage, the new team. Easier said than done. One retiring president told me he had to literally grip his desk and grimace as he sat and watched, mostly from the sidelines, some of the practices and decisions being made by the new team.

An external sale can present its own problems. I have observed the gusto with which the most senior leaders of the acquired firm have been dismissed in the early months after a sale, given they had evolved into more administrative roles or functions that overlapped with the structures already in place at the purchaser's firm (i.e., redundant positions). That approach can remove the most experienced and respected leaders, which subsequently can rapidly change the culture and erode the credibility of the merged firm. Moving too quickly to replace former leaders with less capable candidates can accelerate the decline of a newly acquired asset.

I have also observed many challenges associated with conflicting egos in merged firms. I have learned that it's important to invest enough time to fully understand the egos and levels of self-awareness amongst key individuals in the merged entity. It's also important to observe and be able to separate your own and others' egos from a deal. That will enhance the opportunity for positive outcomes.

To avoid or minimize potential difficulties, you, as a leader, should take the following steps:

- Ensure you inspire and empower your team to grow, develop, and stay with your firm, regardless of the chosen successional path.

- Be honest and empathetic with team members.

- Plan the succession of your firm, assuming an internal sale, but expect you may require an external sale to ensure access to the true value of your firm and to assure the stability and further development of your former firm and team.

- Ensure you understand the stages of the sale process and set your expectations accordingly (e.g., indication of interest, expression of interest, draft sale and purchase agreement, draft consolidated business plan, draft integration plan with predetermined and well-defined roles and responsibilities).

- Don't commit to exclusive negotiations with one potential purchaser until you are confident that the fit will be successful, especially culturally—the purchasers will try to resist this approach but stand firm.

- Carefully consider how the culture of individual entities will be merged.

- Ensure you have looked carefully at separate components of your business that might benefit from being carved off before the sale (e.g., research and prototypes, special projects and long-term investments, insurance-policy assets).

- Use the best advisors and specialists to craft the deal; don't leave anything to chance and make sure you understand every financial, legal, and accounting aspect of the negotiations (regardless of whether you are an architect, engineer, ecologist, planner, etc.).

- Clearly understand what you are getting into and keep detailed records of all discussions, including formal and informal commitments (e.g., document all calls, meetings, commitments).

- Ensure all important elements are clearly spelled out in writing (e.g., employment agreements, roles and responsibilities, the potential for any sale-price adjustments upon close and in subsequent payments, if applicable).

- Ensure you accept no less than 60 percent of the final sale price upon closing, ideally more.

- Settle on a one- or two-year payout of any remaining amounts.

- Understand any non-competition provisions that a buyer may try to impose (i.e., from legal, financial, and ethical perspectives).

- Add interest charges to any future payment amounts held back after the deal closes.

- Ensure all promises, or commitments are supported with written documentation.

Key Points and Observations in Chapter 5:

Managing and Delivering High-Quality, Credible Work

1. Good project management requires common sense, patience, discretion, self-discipline, people skills, and, above all, an attitude of professionalism.

2. If you want your work to be well regarded and to stand up to client and regulatory scrutiny, implement a clear and effective Excellence Assurance/Excellence Empowerment Program (EA/EE).

3. Be prepared for anything in consulting, regardless of legitimacy.

4. Make sure you don't choose to bid on a project if it's only to satisfy your ego or to foolishly chase the odds, hoping that more work will come in. Develop relationships—don't play a fool's game.

5. Under current and standard procurement rules, expect that public bids will erode the profitability of your firm.

6. Firms that are transforming their marketing approaches and thinking differently will outpace those that depend upon typically stale and cookie-cutter approaches.

7. The global racial-awareness movement has presented an opportunity to carefully examine individual and corporate biases and to develop and implement a plan that will embrace a diversity of perspectives across gender, race, belief systems, culture, and age.

8. Giving back is part of the character of the most successful consulting firms. It's an opportunity for companies to connect team members with the communities in which they work. When a company is working on purpose and the team members are in alignment with that purpose, positive business outcomes are the unintended results.

9. Ensure you inspire and empower your team to grow, develop, and stay with your firm, regardless of your firm's successional path.

Chapter 6

Becoming an Enlightened Consultant

IN THE PREVIOUS CHAPTER, I BEGAN TO INTRODUCE SOME OPPORTUNI-
ties for transforming key aspects of a consulting business. Some specific
opportunities were highlighted where firms will thrive when they depart
from egoic thinking and actions. This chapter begins at the roots of a consulting firm's success, with the individual consultant.

As an individual, you may already have reached a point in your own life
where you are self-aware and able to clearly observe the role that your ego
plays in your personal and professional life. This chapter explores where
you can advance your individual interests and your career direction.

Have you invested time exploring and considering your ethics and
values? Have you asked yourself what is most important to you, and if you
are you honouring and respecting your priorities? Looking at a typical
week, do you find yourself living with predominantly positive emotions
or are more negative emotions consuming your energy (see Chapter 2,
Figure 1)?

Early in my career, I was quite ambitious and anxious to quickly climb
up the proverbial corporate ladder. I waited, frequently impatiently, for
my managers and directors to recognize and promote my skills and role.
It seemed the culture, in some firms in particular, was less than innovative and inspiring, allowing and encouraging staff to compete head-on

internally rather than collaborating in order to compete externally. Some firms seem to protect and perpetuate a hierarchical structure that promotes self-interest and selfish behaviours and attitudes.

I was always appreciative and respectful of the leader of the consulting firm with which I first worked. John Gartner (co-founder of Gartner Lee Limited) always treated his staff with respect, regardless of role and status. He was a kind and thoughtful leader and had significant professionalism and integrity.

I started to wonder early in my career about whether there were many consulting firms where team members were valued and rewarded for positive characteristics and behaviours. Surely there was a place where decisions were made that considered more than impacts on revenues and costs and where important, less tangible features and characteristics were actively considered, such as client and staff loyalty, technical credibility, collaboration, innovation, and internal investments (not costs). And surely, making a positive difference within the communities that we worked in was an important ingredient of success.

More recently, as I have explored and advanced my own level of self-awareness, I have also begun to see people and situations more clearly than I did in the past. Hindsight in 2020 was real to me. I reached a level of self-awareness where I can more clearly see what is behind the behaviours and reactions of colleagues, clients, regulators, and competitors. It's almost like a cloud of fog between me and the people I interact with has been lifted. I can observe people and how they behave without taking their words and actions personally.

I had never been asked about self-awareness—it wasn't something I was taught about in school. Later in my career, after encountering some significant bumps in the road both personally and professionally, I began to think that I might not have understood what is truly important to accomplish here, inside, and outside of the office. As I have deepened my knowledge base and experience, I have continued to move toward and apply more wisdom to my daily thoughts and activities.

It's important to shift from broad discussions about your ethics and values to more specific questions, including, Are you happy in your current role and company? If you hesitate before answering, then that may be an indication of where your heart and mind are. Is your leadership (if you aren't the leader) enlightened and aware of and actively promoting your interests and your shift towards a deeper level of self-awareness? Do you feel supported, visible, and valued?

I was struck by one example earlier in my career, where I experienced an unenlightened response from consulting leaders. My spouse worked with the Ontario provincial government at a time when the province was decentralizing government offices and ministries; the intention was to disperse government offices (and jobs) more equitably across the province. That meant a move for her to a location about a two-hour drive from our home at that time.

After much research, I proposed to my senior leaders, who had recently taken their new positions as part of an internal successional plan, that I go to the office three days each week and spend two days a week in our new location, working remotely to allow my spouse and me to continue with our respective careers. I agreed to cover all personal costs to stay locally during those three days at the office, and I committed to making that arrangement work. I also added that I would expand our corporate interests in a new local market. Making it work would allow our spousal careers to continue and our relationship and family to remain intact.

The response back from the company was a firm no—my job required that I be present in the office five days a week. That short-sighted and unempathetic response prompted me (and my ego) to accept an offer to join, and enthusiastically and significantly grow, a competing firm. That experience also contributed to my creation of an entirely remotely based firm later in my career, in 2006 (Savanta). That unconventional initiative emphasized the importance of helping consultants and their families eliminate and reduce commuting time in favour of more balanced lifestyles. It's hard to imagine a leader taking such a short-sighted stance today, as many firms are exploring remote working during the COVID-19 pandemic.

As a consultant, advancing your own self-awareness will contribute significantly to

- observing and identifying egos and emotional responses that are negative and likely ill informed;
- attracting people (colleagues, clients, regulators) who share your positive energy, values, and interests;
- identifying human barriers to individual and team success; and
- identifying and implementing effective team strategies.

Having a solid understanding of your own ethics and values will help you determine how best to interact in challenging scenarios.

How do you know if your current consulting company is where you belong, or where you are meant to be? It's not an easy question to answer. Intuition and your emotions will be of great assistance to you as you ask and answer that question. Intuition is your ability to understand something immediately, without conscious reasoning. You may already intuitively know whether you are in the right company and within the right business sector. Are you spending most of your time experiencing positive emotions? Do you enjoy your work, and does it bring you happiness?

To what degree have you sought to increase your own self-awareness and to identify the role your ego plays in determining how you respond to situations on a day-to-day basis? Do you spend time each day meditating and enjoying some alone and quiet time? It is in those spaces between your mind's active thoughts where your awareness and self-understanding may grow more freely.

Being present allows you to immerse yourself in the activities of the moment. It doesn't allow you to dwell in the past or worry about the future. Planning for and dreaming about your ideal job is completely reasonable, as that allows you to consider whether you are currently fulfilling your purpose. Many gifted leaders and teachers speak eloquently about our reason for being here and the importance of finding the purpose of our lives (e.g., Roman 1989; Dyer 2006; Lakhiani 2016).

As a team member, you should be interested in, and you deserve, a well-defined and reasonably flexible career path. That path should be co-developed with the company, and consistently implemented, and subject to periodic formal and informal reviews and supportive mentoring (i.e., instead of stiff and routine annual reviews). Individuals will benefit from more than a workplace with ping-pong tables, pinball games, comfy couches, and all-you-can-eat Friday afternoons. Individuals who want to grow in a meaningful way are interested in building their skills and better understanding themselves. Those individuals will benefit from a supportive, progressive, and deliberate shift towards greater individual and collective self-awareness.

I have had the pleasure of exploring a couple of tools to help me and my consulting teams enhance our individual and collective awareness and our ability to collaborate successfully with other team members. Two approaches I have found most useful and effective are the Birkman Method and Insights Discovery.

The Birkman Method is a science-backed suite of self-assessment tools that interpret personality data at work and in life. The method is rooted in science, validity, and positive psychology.

Insights Discovery brings self-awareness to people, teams, leaders, and organizations. It helps people increase their self-awareness, allowing them to form better relationships and become more effective at their jobs. The Insights Discovery website notes that "self-understanding is transformative for people; self-aware people are transformative for business."

I immersed myself in the Insights Discovery process and subsequently had my entire team go through the same exercise. I have also taken myself and my team through the Birkman Method personality test. Both methods enabled me to begin to understand my interactions and relations more fully with clients, colleagues, regulators, and a diversity of stakeholders. According to my Insights profile, I'm a directing motivator and an inspiring motivator.

I found it particularly helpful to have trained and certified managers lead those initiatives. There was a mix of responses from the team members who undertook both exercises. Some were not at all interested in participating; the majority, though, were curious and interested in learning more about themselves to improve their communications with their colleagues. I would encourage consultants to look at the Birkman Method and Insights Discovery and other similar types of exercises that may contribute to self-awareness. I would also suggest reading a few books that I found resonated most powerfully with me (e.g., Roman 1989; Tolle 2011; Chugh 2018).

Having your own personal–professional plan that aligns with the general company-wide interests and plans can be a helpful guide and a reminder to stay on your path. Your plan should address:

- Areas you believe you can contribute to your employer in a positive manner (e.g., innovative idea development and implementation).
- An agreed-upon utilization target for the next year, where applicable.
- Your goals related to
    - preferred project types;
    - diversity of projects you are interested in (size, sector, geography);
    - knowledge development (i.e., courses and training);
    - marketing and visibility (e.g., your attendance at conferences, tradeshows, presentations, or technical/trade publication article writing);
    - how you will enhance your self-awareness on an ongoing basis;
    - planned growth and evolution of your role; and
    - compensation.

Maister (1993) offers details about the more traditional how-to aspects of the consulting firm. He raises other questions that may merit some consideration:

- In what way are you personally more valuable in the marketplace than last year?
- What are your plans to make yourself more valuable in the marketplace?

- What specific new skills do you plan to acquire or enhance in the next year?

- What can you do to make yourself (even more) special in the marketplace over the next year?

As you develop your self-awareness, you should test your thoughts around your current role and employer. From your more self-aware perspective, you will better understand the types of people you work alongside and their communication approaches and management styles. You will begin to see more clearly why they take certain positions and approaches (e.g., in many cases, negative, ego-driven positions are underlain by a depth of fear).

You will begin to observe what role their egos play in decision-making, and you will be able to determine how best to work with people driven by egoic thinking, or you may clearly see that you are working with a team of colleagues that have a less than positive and inspiring energy. You will begin to have glimpses of or increase your interest in more authentic relationships.

Advancing your self-awareness and understanding those with whom you work will help you to decide whether you are working with the right team. The marketplace for skilled, self-aware individuals and leaders is open and growing—it's likely that there will be significant team-member movements between firms over the coming months and years. Many will decide to shed the golden handcuffs of share ownership and/or staged incentive bonusing to engage in a more inspiring and aware business model.

It's truly an exciting moment for consultants interested in making more meaningful contributions while attracting significant happiness and abundance into their lives.

Key Points and Observations in Chapter 6:

Becoming an Enlightened Consultant

1. Invest time exploring and considering your ethics and values and determining what is most important to you. Assess whether you are spending most of your time experiencing positive or negative emotions.

2. As a team member, you deserve a well-defined and reasonably flexible career path. That path should be co-developed with the company, consistently implemented, and subject to periodic formal and informal reviews and supportive mentoring.

3. Having your own personal–professional strategy that aligns with the general company-wide interests and plans can be a helpful guide and a reminder to stay on your path.

4. Individuals will benefit from a supportive, progressive, and deliberate shift towards greater personal and collective self-awareness.

5. The marketplace for skilled, self-aware individuals and leaders is open and growing—it's likely that there will be significant team-member movements between firms over the coming months and years.

6. We are amid a truly extraordinary moment in the transformation of the consulting industry, where individuals and companies can create more meaningful contributions.

Chapter 7

The Enlightened Consulting Firm

IF YOU WANT YOUR FIRM TO BE MORE SUCCESSFUL, WHETHER YOU ARE an owner or not, and if you want to attract more self-aware and positive contributors to your firm, understand and honestly answer the following questions:

- Is your firm genuine, warm, and welcoming? *Blue square traditional*

- Do the people you have met or have worked with seem authentic, or do they seem more distracted and/or superficial?

- Are recruiters and human resources staff inspired and encouraging? Is human resources considered an important and relevant aspect in your firm? (Note: Some firms consider human resources to simply be a box to check to ensure compliance; they don't understand the transformative power and influence of many in that profession).

- Does your firm support its employees (beyond being allowed to go to conferences and courses)? Do they actively promote meaningful self-awareness training and support?

- Does your firm have thoughtful and transparent hiring practices and incentives to increase diversity in all forms?

- Is your firm inclusive and supportive of members of BIPOC (Black, Indigenous, People of Colour) communities?

- Does your firm offer well-paid internships (not volunteer or below living-wage positions) that recognize the importance of engaging future consultants and leaders?

- Is your firm's website clear in terms of key information (e.g., vision, mission, degree of awareness and enlightenment), and is it actively and routinely managed and updated?

- Is your firm completing interesting and meaningful work?

- Does your firm respect and reward staff in a helpful, flexible, and creative manner?

- Is your compensation package fair and equitable, and are the bonus and benefit programs transparent, generous, and inclusive?

Each of you, whether leaders or members of a consulting team, will have some of the answers to these questions. Together a firm should be able to determine where it falls on the continuum from unaware to enlightened. As you work through this exercise, you will understand the work that needs to be done and where priorities lie to ensure your company remains aware, viable, and sustainable over time.

Hams (2012) speaks to the common characteristics of great companies:

- They care deeply about their team members, their services, and their clients;

- They have fun; and

- They have high expectations of performance.

Moving from great to enlightened companies means additional emphasis on

- inspired vision and leadership;

- inspired and engaged team members; and

- respectful, genuine, and honest dialogue.

An Inspired Vision and Leadership

Traditional measures of a consulting firm's success focus on effectively managing the flow and the delivery of work, while getting paid for that work and generating a reasonable profit margin. It's that simple: Find the work, deliver it, get paid, and ensure you keep the flow of work coming through.

There are some different aspects to defining success in a more enlightened firm. And regardless of the size and nature of a firm, there is also one ingredient that is essential: an inspired vision.

A firm's inspired vision needs to address

- meaningful outcomes;
- acceptance and encouragement of increased diversity (gender, race, culture, age);
- more genuine and complete models of collaboration and integration across technical disciplines and across traditional hierarchical levels;
- the cultivation of positive energy and associated emotions; and
- the promotion of more balanced lifestyles amongst staff.

Leaders need to be able to communicate that vision with clarity and passion in order to truly lead their teams.

Brady and Woodward (2013) state: *"Leaders lead for the joy of creating something bigger than themselves."* Their leadership is about

- giving power;
- helping others; and
- serving others.

Some people (and their egos) see leadership being about gaining power and control, accessing perks, or being served. More authentic, enlightened leadership is about connecting with people, being truthful, embracing empathy, and focusing on elevating all the members of a team and the team as a whole.

Leadership is best expressed with an attitude of humility. A true leader quietly and patiently helps team members grow, supporting and encouraging the growth of their self-awareness and empowering them to make conscious, inclusive decisions. Authentic and more enlightened leaders humbly prefer to share credit or let the teams take the credit for important and meaningful advances.

Some consultants and traditional consulting firms have a more cynical perspective on some of these enlightenment indicators, suggesting that younger generations are less effective and suffer from a sense of entitlement. "They don't work as hard as we worked," some lament. That cynical response will cause the persistence of intolerant thinking and the inability of many firms to keep up with rapidly changing clients and markets. That's a disadvantage for most firms but a significant advantage for the smaller number of firms that choose to become more aware and progressive.

Being progressive creates space for innovation, which embraces thinking differently about every aspect of the consulting business. Leading firms and emerging leaders in the industry need to more fully understand and properly address innovation, diversity (gender, race, culture, age), inclusiveness, practical and meaningful outcomes, the importance, and application of wisdom, and a higher than typical measure of creativity.

Consultants need to support one another in the industry and to help each other awaken to our singular and collective strengths and wisdom. We need to be able to understand, identify, and manage our egos to ensure we operate from an enlightened and grounded perspective.

My experience has led me to understand that thought leadership is also an important ingredient in an enlightened firm. It helps differentiate your firm from others and significantly improves business outcomes. Individuals and firms that embrace thought leadership are more sought after and are typically engaged earlier in projects and processes.

Thought leaders are knowledgeable and informed. They are leaders in their fields of expertise in part because they can tap into talent, experience, and wisdom to consistently answer the larger questions on the minds of a particular target audience. They may be leaders who address how technical advances affect certain specialized areas of study, or they may be thought leaders at a more corporate or visionary scale, answering questions across an industry or about global trends. Some of the questions that always seem to be part of my own internal dialogue include the following:

- Where is a particular market headed?
- How will changes in technology and governance alter industries and leading consulting firms?
- Is there a need for market consolidation and integration of expertise?
- Has the time arrived for the behemoths to fragment and disintegrate into more effective, more nimble, smaller, and more local organizations?

Leaders need to be more open and less me-first sales-oriented to truly inspire team members. Individuals need to understand the importance of their roles, without cute, patronizing, and, in some cases, demeaning labels. Labelling and name calling seems to have become the norm in some jurisdictions where some political leaders use or tolerate juvenile name calling to denigrate the character and integrity of individuals, companies, communities, and other countries. It's disappointing to see these attitudes perpetuated and enabled in some areas of the consulting industry. And it's time for those attitudes, where they persist, to change.

Inspired and Engaged Team Members

People (e.g., clients, colleagues, regulators) increase the complexity of consulting. More enlightened firms are those that will understand and work with people who have a diversity of perspectives.

Staff is a term most consulting companies use; I prefer the terms team members or colleagues to reduce the unnecessary imposition or reminder of a hierarchy. Unlike many leaders who are heavily invested in egoic thinking, team members are especially interested in a service leadership model, which actively promotes

- an understandable company vision and a picture of how and where team members fit within an organization (no one likes to get over-looked, misunderstood, or pigeon-holed);
- honesty in all internal and external dialogue;
- equity and inclusiveness;
- a consistent commitment to excellence and innovation; and
- strategic planning for the future of the firm and for the future of team members' careers.

I believe in service leadership, a term I use intentionally. The term servant leadership has been widely used and applied. It has appropriately fallen out of favour as the term servant is understood by many as a reference to a Black domestic servant, a term rooted deeply in racism. The current and rapid movement away from racist brands and racist thinking amongst informed companies and individuals is evidence of a transformative awakening happening around the world. These movements and marches are vocally and widely addressing centuries of oppression and a culture of White privilege and greed. It's well past time for this transformation and the shift towards acknowledging and accepting responsibility for the perpetuation of racism and oppression.

Ward and Wiley (2020) speak about this current trend in their article titled, "14 Racist Brands, Mascots, and Logos That Were Considered Just Another Part of American Life." They refer to how "White Southerners once used 'uncle' and 'aunt' as honorifics for older Blacks because they refused to say 'Mr.' and 'Mrs.'" Hence the recent announcements about the corporate review and evolution of brands such as Uncle Ben's and Aunt Jemima.

Beyond moving away from racist and oppressive language, we also need to stop labelling our team members with simplistic terms like sellers (rainmakers, finders), minders (managers, project managers), and doers (grinders). Maister (1993) uses three other types of client work to help define the structure of organizations and where individuals might fit: brain, grey hair, and procedural projects. These terms can also be understood by some to be offensive and can be interpreted by team members as demeaning and patronizing.

Some managers and leaders use these labels to try to add some buzz and internal competition amongst staff. The trend towards turning doers into sellers (Kienle 2019) and the widespread use of a seller–doer model perpetuates the homogenous herd mentality around many aspects of consulting operations and sales.

Respectful, Genuine, and Honest Dialogue

Enlightened companies foster an environment where open and honest dialogue can be entered into with team members, asking questions that may seem outside of a particular technical role, such as the following:

- Are you happy in our firm?
- How would you describe working in our firm (e.g., rewarding, meaningful, frustrating, irritating)?
- As your manager, what have I done to help or hinder your job performance? What can I do to help you do your job better?
- Do you have the resources and tools you need to perform your job?
- What accomplishment(s) are you most proud of?
- What have you found most challenging?

So how do we inspire our consultants and consulting teams and excite them about the roles they play? We do that by actively listening to them and by thinking differently.

Active listening engages all our senses and involves making a conscious decision to pay close attention to verbal and non-verbal cues. As we listen, we should remain non-judgemental and resist leaping in, to challenge or test words and thoughts being expressed. Exercise patience and tolerance as you listen; don't jump to your own conclusions.

In a few cases, I have found using a talking stick to be helpful, especially in emotionally charged meetings and events. Used in many Indigenous cultures, a talking stick can encourage and ensure effective communications. It can foster a level of respect during meetings. The person holding the stick is the only one who may speak; all others must listen respectfully.

Grounding a firm with inspired vision and leadership, promoting and supporting inspired and engaged team members, and engaging with colleagues in a respectful, genuine, and honest manner will optimize success, and it will move a firm and its team towards enlightenment.

Key Points and Observations in Chapter 7:

The Enlightened Consulting Firm

1. Moving from great to enlightened companies means additional emphasis on

   - inspired vision and leadership;

   - inspired and engaged team members; and

   - respectful, genuine, and honest dialogue.

2. Leadership is best expressed with an attitude of humility; a true leader quietly and patiently helps team members grow, supporting and encouraging the growth of their self-awareness and empowering them to make conscious, inclusive decisions.

3. Authentic and more enlightened leaders humbly prefer to share credit or let the teams take the credit for important and meaningful advances.

4. Some consultants and traditional consulting firms have a more cynical perspective on indicators of an individual or a firm's enlightenment. That cynical response will cause the persistence of intolerant thinking and the inability of those firms to keep up with rapidly changing clients and markets.

5. Innovation means thinking differently about every aspect of the consulting business.

6. Leading firms and emerging leaders in the industry need to more fully understand and properly address innovation, diversity (gender, race, culture, age), inclusiveness, practical and meaningful outcomes, the importance and application of wisdom, and a higher than typical measure of creativity.

7. It's well beyond time to put an end to the use of unenlightened language and the use of racist and oppressive language and demeaning terms.

8. Grounding a firm with inspired vision and leadership, promoting and supporting inspired and engaged team members, and engaging with colleagues in a respectful, genuine, and honest manner will optimize success, and it will move a firm and its team towards enlightenment.

Chapter 8

Leading Industry Trends and Emerging Markets— An Enlightened Perspective

ENLIGHTENED FIRMS LOOK FORWARD TO WHERE MARKETS ARE headed. They position their firms and individual consultants to be leaders and knowledge experts in emerging markets. They invest in building teams and tools that will support that leadership.

The consulting industry is changing rapidly in and is causing some leaders and firms to look ahead of market curves. Some of the emerging markets summarized in this chapter are growing rapidly, and some will be subject to adjustments, acquisition, and consolidation initiatives.

The following are key, transformative issues and challenges that are changing the face of consulting:

- the role of new and emerging technologies;
- climate change, resiliency, and adaptation;
- sustainability and sustainable development; and
- the circular economy.

The Role of New and Emerging Technologies

Early in my career, before cellphones, fax machines, and word processing that wasn't on a conventional typewriter, the world seemed more reasonably paced. Technology has significantly increased the speed of commerce, and it has enabled consultants to successfully complete consulting projects and associated correspondence and reports much more rapidly and simply. I know I date myself with comments like this, but in my early days in the consulting industry, a simple typo on a page could cause a re-type of pages and/or documents. Significant efficiencies were and continue to be gained through the adoption of new technologies. I was an early adopter of mobile phones and have tried my best to research, source out, and use the best technologies throughout my career.

In 2006, when I created Savanta, I decided that we would establish our platform based on Apple equipment. That was during a period when Apple technologies and hardware were coveted for their aesthetic design and their technical capabilities. The choice involved a substantial investment, but the Savanta team members appreciated the ability to work with and depend on higher-end design and technology. Such decisions are taken after careful consideration of optimizing costs, but in the case of Savanta, the cost became an investment in staff and a strategic investment in differentiating our firm from others.

Interestingly, Apple Canada recorded our hardware launch in one of its Apple stores, before opening time. That included an interview and the production of a professional video that promoted the relationship between Apple Canada and Savanta. That video is apparently still used inside Apple for business promotion and training purposes. As a small and innovative firm, we were honoured to be profiled by an extraordinarily innovative and massively successful firm.

Other areas of active technological change currently affecting the environmental consulting industry include environmental DNA (eDNA), an inexpensive and time-efficient approach to finding DNA in the environment. eDNA originates from material shed by organisms into aquatic or terrestrial environments. It can be sampled and monitored using new molecular test methods. These sampling methods enable more rapid and cost-effective data collection relevant to species distribution and relative abundance. For species that are difficult to detect (e.g., rare and endangered), eDNA provides a comparatively improved alternative method and catch-per-unit effort (United States Geological Survey 2020).

A review of other technologies suggests that many will optimize environmental data collection, including ongoing improvements to drone technologies (e.g., battery life, payload capacity) along with remote cameras, Wi-Fi, thermal imaging, heat maps, and data analytics.

Savanta decided in 2015 to carefully examine and consider how technology could improve the efficiency and effectiveness of traditional ecological field-data collection. That decision was part of our "think differently" approach to consulting. We developed our first app, Red Squirrel, working collaboratively with a prominent software development company, and with the leading branding company Field Trip & Co. to create an impactful software package. A promotional handout developed for this app highlighted its features:

In a Nutshell

- *Red Squirrel is an iOS app developed by Savanta Inc. and TribalScale Inc.*
- *It enables the rapid collection and digitization of data that typically takes much longer to manually record*
- *Red Squirrel relies on fillable templated forms developed for the iPad*

- *The app is supported by a master list of over 8,000 wildlife and plant species*
- *The master lists highlight species at risk to allow field ecologists to note critical habitat characteristics while they are still in the field*

Tangible Advantages

- *Increased efficiency and reduced data collection costs*
- *Flexible and mobile*
- *Encourages consistent data collection practices amongst field staff*
- *Transcription errors are eliminated*
- *Sampling locations can be precisely pinpointed*
- *Field survey routes can be mapped*
- *Images and sounds can be captured*
- *Output includes report-ready summary data tables*
- *Seamless storage to a server eliminating lost/misplaced data sheets*

Red Squirrel's Special Features:

- *Species at risk (SAR) alerts*
- *Google Map view of the project area*
- *One-tap UTM coordinate recording*
- *Handy dropdown menus*
- *Data validation with mandatory fields*
- *Autofill weather conditions*
- *Photo attachments with location information (UTM coordinates) and pins*

Artificial intelligence (AI) is an emerging technology that I admit I know little about. I understand that AI makes it possible for machines to learn from experience and perform human-like tasks. The environmental branch of consulting engages large numbers of consultants in various data collection and analysis initiatives. Some branches of this field (e.g., meteorology, hydrogeology, landscape ecology) are relying more on modelling and associated applications to try to answer complicated questions related to large-scale changes. I leave this topic for subsequent, more detailed, and comprehensive discussions outside of this book.

Climate Change, Resiliency, and Adaptation

Our world is changing quickly, and our responses to key issues have not yet caught up to the momentum and magnitude of change. Climate change is a significant concern. Gough (2017) notes that the hazards of uncontrolled climate change constitute an *"epochal threat-multiplier"* that will make the pursuit of economic and social rights more difficult. He states that if global warming exceeds the 2°C threshold, it will overwhelm all attempts to eradicate poverty, reduce global security, and impact the persistence of flourishing human life.

The Paris Agreement, a common and global response to the threat of climate change, is based upon keeping a rise in global temperature this century to well below 2°C above pre-industrial levels. Noteworthy is the absence in the agreement of what those pre-industrial levels are (King, Henley, and Hawkins 2017). It's hard to imagine any informed and intelligent people and governments remaining in denial of the science behind and the ongoing real-world impacts of climate change.

Parties to the Paris Agreement acknowledge that *"adaptation action should follow a country-driven, gender-responsive, participatory, and fully transparent approach, considering vulnerable groups, communities and ecosystems, and should be based on and guided by the best available science and,* as appropriate, traditional knowledge, knowledge of Indigenous peoples and local knowledge systems, with a view to integrating adaptation into relevant socioeconomic and environmental policies and actions" (United Nations Framework Convention on Climate Change 2020).

Only four countries on this planet are not signatories to the Paris Accord: Iran, Iraq, Angola, and Libya. The U.S. rejoined on Feb 19, 2021.

Adaptation refers to adjustments in ecological, social, or economic systems in response to actual or expected climatic stimuli and their effects or impacts. It refers to changes in processes, practices, and structures to moderate potential damages or to benefit from opportunities associated with climate change. Both mitigation and adaptation measures are required to address climate change. Mitigation measures will include, for example, reducing fossil fuel extraction, pricing carbon, fostering renewable energy technologies, making changes to rural land use, and managing urban forms and land use (Gough 2017).

The pace of adaptation is lagging behind the changes needed. This rapidly emerging consulting market is substantial, and it will test our ability to be as intelligent, responsive, creative, and resourceful as possible. Not only is the emerging industry large, but it's also leading towards significant and meaningful outcomes. Current leaders in these fields, including several European countries, have an advanced position in this emerging industry.

The political reluctance in the United States over the past few years to even acknowledge the reality of climate change may delay and dampen the development and credibility of the climate change consulting industry in that country. This challenge is countered by the reality of increasing frequency and intensity of wildfires, heatwaves, droughts and storms experienced in that country in 2021.

Sustainability and Sustainable Development

Sustainability means meeting our own needs without compromising the ability of future generations to meet their own needs (Edwards 2005; Woods 2010). The term emerged in the early 1980s and has become a fixture in consulting service offerings from a range of types of consulting firms. I consider this area to include important markets, such as green urbanism, green infrastructure, and green growth.

This market began in earnest in 1987 when the World Commission on Environment and Development published its findings in *Common Future*. The Commission stated that it believes that *"people can build a future that is more prosperous, more just and more secure."* It went on to note, however, that this positive hope for the future is *"conditional on decisive political action now* (i.e., in 1987) *to ensure both sustainable human progress and human survival."*

As we step back and look at where we now stand, after that call for immediate and decisive action almost forty years ago, it is no wonder that there are growing movements and calls for immediate change (e.g., School Strikes for Climate Change led by our youth, most notably Greta Thunberg). Time has passed and our shared crises have deepened. Traditional dependencies on self-interest, greed, and short-term vision have created and fed the increasingly vocal demand for substantial and real change.

Those who are now rising *en masse* are the courageous and important leaders of our new transformative era. They are not to be dismissed as pie-eyed socialists, as some have called them. They are individuals and groups who merit our immediate and full attention and responsive action.

As with any emerging space or market, sustainability represents an opportunity for consultants to review and to reconsider their firm's ability to evolve and adapt to different kinds of needs. In my mind, this points to the urgent and significant opportunity to remake firms for true collaboration. That means suspending expectations that management, planning, design, communications, or engineering-driven firms will alone be able to address these emerging needs.

I encourage you to read and think about Gough's (2017) book *Heat, Greed and Human Need*. It provides a thorough and thoughtful consideration of the role and effects of capitalism in a world where important ecosystem function thresholds have been and are being crossed. We are also observing significant transformations emerging in the economic industry (e.g., work towards the definition of corporate purpose, impact investing, conservation finance). The 2020 Davos Manifesto is subtitled, "The Universal Purpose of a Company in the Fourth Industrial Revolution." It's quite interesting to read the manifesto, which states, in part:

> *The purpose of a company is to engage all its stakeholders in shared and sustained value creation. In creating such value, a company serves not only its shareholders, but all its stakeholders—employees, customers, suppliers, local communities, and society at large. The best way to understand and harmonize the divergent interests of all stakeholders is through a shared commitment to policies and decisions that strengthen the long-term prosperity of a company.*

The consulting industry would be wise to look carefully at the 2020 Davos Manifesto (produced by the World Economic Forum) and the 17 UN Sustainable Development Goals (and associated materials). In my mind, there has never been an emerging market curve so large and so significant; this is truly a market and a time that will challenge all business leaders and will favour enlightened leaders who continually and strategically place their firms ahead of the curve (i.e., at the leading edge of new markets).

Leading-edge consulting firms are not frequently encountered, as that market position requires investments that may lower profitability in the short term. Being at the leading edge isn't a crowded space but occupying it can be tremendously rewarding and can result in meaningful outcomes.

Strategic investments are critical for leading-edge firms, and their leaders need to look non-traditionally at standard accounting labels and methods. It requires thinking about strategic investments as assets, not as fixed or hard costs that need to be constantly constricted. That shift in direction, however, depends upon enlightened and courageous leadership.

The Circular Economy

The circular economy is rapidly causing the redesign of manufacturing and global waste markets. It replaces the traditional throw-away, or end-of-life concept, with restoration, repair, reuse, repurposing, and eventually recycling. This approach to the waste management business will be enhanced using renewable energy, the elimination of toxic chemicals, and the reduction or elimination of waste through the smarter and better design of materials and products.

Whether this approach is taken in a developed or a developing economy, outcomes will be less costly in the long run. Repairing a product made to last will always be less expensive than producing it from scratch. This change in the market will create substantial opportunities for firms that choose to remain at the leading edge of this change.

Key Points and Observations in Chapter 8:

Leading Industry Trends and Emerging Markets—
An Enlightened Perspective

1. Enlightened firms look forward to where markets are headed.

2. Our world is changing quickly, and our responses to key issues have not yet caught up to the momentum and magnitude of change.

3. The pace of climate change adaptation is lagging behind the changes needed. This rapidly emerging consulting market is substantial, and it will test our ability to be as intelligent, responsive, creative, and resourceful as possible.

4. It is no wonder that there are growing movements and calls for immediate change. Our globally shared crises have deepened since the call for immediate and decisive action almost forty years ago (*Our Common Future* 1987).

5. The emerging sustainability market will challenge all business leaders and will favour enlightened leaders who continually and strategically place their firms ahead of the curve. That leading position will include transforming firms and their allies towards true collaboration.

6. Strategic investments require thinking differently about fixed or hard costs that need to be constantly constricted. Enlightened and courageous leadership will see some of these costs as essential investments.

7. The leading edge isn't a crowded space, but it can be tremendously rewarding and can result in more meaningful outcomes.

Chapter 9

Foresight in the 2020s—
The Future of a Transformed Consulting Industry

WHAT DOES THE FUTURE OF THE CONSULTING INDUSTRY LOOK LIKE? In a word: bright. It will continue to grow globally, and the most successful firms leading the industry are those that have already begun to transform and adapt to our rapidly changing world. In this chapter, I offer comments and observations related to the broad consulting industry, with additional specific comments related to the environmental consulting industry.

Traditional structures and attitudes will be replaced over accelerated timeframes by firms that

1. inspire and lead their team members, and
2. work intelligently and respectfully with their clients.

The typical and traditional top-down hierarchical approach to consulting will be replaced with more innovative, integrated (across disciplines and roles), open, and flexible leadership and management models.

What is a fully aware and integrated firm? The answer begins with a better understanding of the relationships between and amongst the environment (the natural features and processes), diverse cultures, communities, and various structures and systems (e.g., financial, governance).

As an ecologist, I have devoted most of my career to studying and understanding the natural environment. It's important for all of us, regardless of our profession, to have a deeper understanding of and appreciation for our shared natural surroundings. We need a better and more complete understanding of how well integrated the environment is in investment and development decisions, and in consulting assignments. We have become quite disconnected from the rhythms and beauty of nature. That disconnection has affected and distorted some of our governance and market-driven systems.

In my career, I have worked with developers, builders, investors, governments, regulators, institutions, environmental non-governmental organizations (ENGOs), decision-makers, and other consultants. I have found that successful outcomes on projects increase when they are based on a comprehensive understanding of the environment and how people and projects integrate and interact with the environment. That understanding begins with an appreciation of the place a project or investment occupies in the landscape. Questions that need to be answered, for example, include the following:

- Is a project or investment prone to increased risk associated with its landscape location (e.g., wave uprush zones, low-lying coastal zones, rising sea levels, floodplains, stable slopes, erosion, availability of potable water and breathable air)?

- Is the location in a coastal, marine and estuarine, or freshwater setting?

- Is the area being examined part of a well-defined surface water catchment?

- How does the project location in a surface catchment affect the physical and biological features, functions, and processes present?

- Are there sensitivities associated with areas of groundwater infiltration or discharge?

- Are areas of groundwater discharge associated only with local topography and infiltration areas, or are they the result of larger-scale or regional landscapes?

- Do human-created origins diminish the importance of natural features?

The COVID-19 pandemic has reminded us that all life on earth is connected. Human, animal, plant, and environmental health and well-being are all connected and profoundly influenced by human activities (Robinson and Walzer 2020). We collectively need to better understand and integrate socioeconomic, political, and environmental factors into our thinking and into our consulting firms and projects. A trans-disciplinary approach that integrates ecosystems and human and cultural health is essential to our ability to improve outcomes.

We are beginning to see more cohesive approaches to people and the environment in emerging areas of consulting, including

- a transition towards sustainable economies (e.g., through environmental, social, and governance factor consideration);

- early initiatives to better understand the value and importance of ecosystem services (in many cases monetizing those services);

- initiatives such as understanding and defining nature's role in the transition to a green economy;

- integrated planning that ensures the participation of all affected stakeholders and that considers all social, economic, and environmental costs and benefits; and

- integrated environmental decision-making that includes an appropriate reliance on the best available scientific information.

Other questions need to be asked in terms of Indigenous peoples and various cultures and communities:

- What communities (traditional and current) might be affected by projects and investments?

- Have these communities been involved or included in dialogue and design around a project?

- Has meaningful consultation been completed and have respectful relationships been built?

- Has an investment or project been given free, prior, and informed consent by the Indigenous peoples and their leaders? Are outcomes being appropriately shared and distributed?

- In terms of potential cultural effects, has culture been adequately defined and understood?

- Has a fulsome understanding been built of obligations, responsibilities, and relationships with the land?

Once a comprehensive understanding of environmental, cultural, social, and economic factors is completed, then the emerging and evolving areas of finance (e.g., ecosystem goods and services, natural capital, impact investing, and forest ecosystem goods and services) can be considered. Various national governments along with the following institutions are currently immersed in areas of financial innovation:

- The Economics of Ecosystems and Biodiversity;

- European Commission;

- European Academies Science Advisory Council; and

- International Science-Policy Platform on Biodiversity and Ecosystem Services.

The following table (Figure 3) provides an example checklist of a broad range of natural functions, processes, features, risks, and ecosystem services that can be used to ensure a more comprehensive understanding of the biophysical environment, regardless of types of development projects and investments. Again, the list is not intended to be all inclusive, but I have found it to be helpful in my efforts to better define, understand, and measure environmental features, function, and linkages.

1. TERRAIN SETTING
- Arctic
- Boreal
- Montane
- Major forest biomes (taiga, temperate, tropical)
- Great Plains
- Desert and Semi-Desert
- Coastal and Marine
- Meso-American
- Caribbean

2. REGULATING SERVICES
- Carbon sequestration and storage
- Local climate and air quality
- Moderation of risks (e.g., floods, storms)
- Erosion prevention
- Pollination

3. WATER

Groundwater
- Ground water discharge—headwaters (ground and surface water interactions)
- Ground water recharge—seasonal or permanent
- Ground water quality and temperature

Surface Water
- Watershed, subwatershed/catchment location

Conveyance
- Floodwater and flow regulation, storage
- Erosion control, shoreline stabilization, sediment stabilization

Quality and Temperature Effects
- Sediment/toxicant reduction and retention
- Organic contributions—invertebrates and debris
- Biogeochemical processes—cycling, removal, and/or storage

---

4. LAND AND BIOTA

General
- Decomposition processes
- Biological diversity
- Community structure
- Species richness
- Productivity
- Soil formation
- Fire regime
- Specialized habitats

Seasonal Concentration Areas
- Area-dependent
- Colonial nesting
- Mangroves
- Seagrass
- Dunes
- Winter mammal cover
- Amphibian habitat
- Reptile habitat
- Seeps and springs
- Alvar habitat

---

5. SPECIAL FEATURES
- Vegetation communities at risk
- Species at risk
- Vegetation community scarcity

6. LINKAGES

- Riparian
- Marine, estuarine
- Cross-terrain

7. SOCIO-CULTURAL

- Productive
- Consumptive
- Recreation, passive
- Wellness
- Traditional values and rights

8. AGE, DEGREE OF DISTURBANCE

- Long-term landscape presence
- Settlement period creation or alteration
- Recent history/creation
- Historical and cultural importance

9. VIABILITY AND RESILIENCE

- Source and sustainability of water
- Flood damage prevention
- Resilience of vegetation and wildlife

Figure 3: checklist of natural functions, processes, features, risks, and ecosystem services

These shifts towards a more comprehensive understanding (including linkages and inter-relationships) and integration of the biophysical environment will negatively affect firms that are dependent upon typical or traditional approaches and ideas. Firms dominated by one or two disciplines (e.g., civil engineering, planning, management) will start to slow down, eventually losing their prominence in various business sectors.

The environmental consulting firms that will rise are those that are more innovative and adaptable with a fully integrated blend of traditional and emerging technical disciplines. Those emerging disciplines and technical areas of study include

- authentic engagement and collaboration with Indigenous peoples;
- climate change resiliency and adaptation;
- green/natural infrastructure design and implementation;
- eco-health;
- ecopsychology;
- ecosystem recovery and ecological restoration/rewilding;
- comprehensive social and/or cultural impact assessment;
- genuine and fulsome engagement with stakeholders and communities;
- sustainable development and technologies; and
- economics of ecosystems and biodiversity.

It's also likely, given the proven and projected growth in the environmental consulting industry, that larger management consulting firms will more intentionally try to enter into the environmental consulting space through various strategic and geographic acquisitions. We are likely to see a cycle of integration of mid-sized environmental firms into larger management consulting firms, as management firms seek new ways to evolve and grow.

Coincident with that cycle will be an increasing fragmentation of the behemoths where many more individuals and entire teams will leave to create their own enterprises. These actions will in part be driven by a quest by many younger and other, more self-aware consultants to embrace or step into a more enlightened role within a more enlightened consulting firm.

The merger and acquisition markets will see diminished successes without a thorough and critical assessment (without egoic thinking) of how the new merged entities will function. That assessment will include implementing measures that will keep merged entities ahead of ongoing environmental, economic, social, and governance changes. Change will continue to be the new normal in the consulting industry. Change and resiliency will continue to favour success in enlightened companies.

Many factors will continue to affect the predicted rate of growth in this industry. The politics of nations and communities can set the short-term general tone regarding environmental conservation, restoration, and remediation activities and can affect the projects and associated revenues available to the consulting industry.

The recent shift towards the political far-right wing in some countries has emphasized a diminished importance attached to the natural environment (including diverse peoples and cultures dependent upon the environment), coincident with a preference for streamlined rules and accelerated, more efficient approaches to environmental conservation. In some cases, this shift is occurring too rapidly and recklessly. Right-wing reactions tend to be exaggerated after periods of more centrist and left-leaning governments and environmental policies, which have tended to oppress many types of development.

This right-leaning political shift in some parts of the world has dismissed attention to, or disregarded as mythology, emerging areas of considerable international scientific attention and business investment (e.g., climate change). The International Institute for Environment and Development

(IIED) director Andrew Norton has commented that *"increasing nation-alism and xenophobia mask destructive interests that threaten both planet and people, eroding the solidarity needed for effective global action. And time is short: from the climate crisis to biodiversity loss, any delay in reaction is potentially catastrophic"* (IIED 2019).

The oppression of development has not always been based upon the best science, but rather, it's frequently inappropriately based upon self-interest and not-in-my-backyard (NIMBY) attitudes and preferences. Some might even suggest that this has become a NIABY (not in anyone's backyard) syndrome. The shift towards and away from environmental protection and enhancement is not new. Successive government administrations (and their supporting stakeholders) can tend to overreact, pushing back against existing policies and approaches.

I have many experiences observing egos in the ENGO side of consulting, as some of those groups line up to battle against resource extraction and community-development projects, rallying crowds of citizens armed with partial and misinformation.

Fear can be a significant driver in local and broader scale opposition to growth. Frequently, a small handful of privileged White people can delay, frustrate, and even derail significant projects. That occurs even in the event proposed projects have gone well beyond traditional approaches to mitigate and minimize impacts and provide overall gains.

I worked on an interesting assignment for a mineral aggregate extraction project that opponents labelled a mega-quarry, given its proposed 937 ha size. It was one of the most innovative projects I have encountered in the mineral-extraction approvals process in Canada. It would have seen a shift from truck transport of stone and gravel resources to a rejuvenated rail system, significantly reducing some social and economic effects. Urban idealists drove the opposition to this innovative assignment, despite it having no impacts on their urban community. Urban locavores complained that the loss of the sandy upland potato production areas would constrain restauranteurs and urban lifestyles. I don't assign blame on anyone in these types of circumstances; it's just sad to see the oppression of innovation resulting from fear-based, ill-informed people and movements.

The characterization of the natural environment and the economics of projects have advanced more rapidly than the measurement and consideration of social-cultural factors. Those social-cultural factors help us to understand the potential impact of legislation, regulations, policies, and projects on potentially affected stakeholders. It's important to note that the primary task of social-impact assessment (SIA) is to improve social and cultural outcomes. SIA should be focused on enhancing the benefits of projects to impacted communities (i.e., not just reducing negative impacts).

Enlightenment and success in the consulting industry will depend upon a firm's ability to fully understand and incorporate environmental, economic, and social aspects of programs and projects. Understanding the relationship amongst natural, social, and economic factors should allow us to better understand opportunities for more positive outcomes, especially amongst more vulnerable and less prioritized members of our communities and societies. All stakeholders in projects implemented by consultants need to be treated with respect, and community engagement needs to be genuine and comprehensive.

The United Nations Guiding Principles on Business and Human Rights helps to guide us in that direction. Indigenous peoples and nations will continue to take a more prominent role in successful outcomes through their ongoing promotion of long overdue and genuine efforts towards reconciliation. Firms and nations that choose to ignore international goals, objectives, rules, and guidelines solely in favour of their own national, regional, local, and self-interests are those that will be exposed to higher risks and will not likely be viable or profitable over time.

Firms and individuals who understand the realities of environmental change will more rapidly and adeptly adjust and advance their consulting models. Those who look for balanced, not extreme, or punitive, outcomes will also benefit.

Like the COVID-19 pandemic, climate change is affecting everything, including the survival of people, countries, and their economies. Climate change deniers and misleading and negative politics in some countries are twisting and disrupting informed perspectives and actions. How do you determine what climate change will do to your business? Again, it's time to think differently. The following questions might help stimulate thinking and planning:

- How much time and energy does your team invest in commuting?

- Does your firm offer business and personal incentives related to electric-vehicle use, bicycles, or mass transit?

- Does your firm incent staff to make changes to their personal practices and behaviours that contribute to greenhouse gas production?

- Do the leaders in your firm lead by example when it comes to obvious behaviours that will limit climate change (e.g., home and office energy efficiency; switch to renewables where available; food consumption, including eating less meat and avoiding food waste; purchasing local to reduce transport impacts; orienting their financial portfolios to align with impact investing)?

Regardless of the emerging complexities in consulting, those who will benefit most in the future are individuals and firms that

- embrace a deeper understanding of our shared, integrated, and interconnected natural environment;
- fully understand and incorporate environmental, economic, and social aspects into programs and projects;
- invest in and lead the integration of traditional and emerging technical disciplines;
- adopt and follow important UN commitments, including Sustainable Development Goals and the United Nations Declaration on the Rights of Indigenous Peoples as a reconciliation framework;
- seek more positive outcomes, especially amongst more vulnerable and less prioritized members of our communities and societies;
- build and foster a character of honesty, authenticity, transparency; and
- lead by example, at both personal and corporate levels.

Key Points and Observations in Chapter 9:

Foresight in the 2020s—
The Future of a Transformed Consulting Industry

1. Traditional hierarchical approaches to consulting will be replaced with more innovative, better integrated, and more open and flexible leadership and management models.

2. All life on earth is connected. We collectively need to better understand and integrate social, cultural, economic, and environmental factors into our thinking and into our consulting firms and projects.

3. Once a comprehensive understanding of the broad environmental factors is established, then the emerging and evolving areas of finance, including ecosystem goods and services, natural capital, and forest ecosystem goods and services can be considered.

4. Firms dominated by one or two disciplines (e.g., civil engineering, planning, management) will slow down and begin to lose their prominence in the consulting industry.

5. Change will continue to be the new normal in the consulting industry. Change and resiliency will continue to favour success in enlightened companies.

6. As we see consolidation continue through mergers and acquisitions, we will see a new wave of fragmentation of larger and mid-sized firms where many more individuals will leave to create their own enterprises. These actions will in part be driven by a quest by many younger and other, more self-aware consultants to embrace or step into a more enlightened role within a more enlightened consulting firm.

7. Enlightenment and success in the consulting industry will depend upon a firm's ability to fully understand and incorporate environmental, social, cultural, and economic aspects of programs and projects.

Chapter 10

Concluding Observations and the Next Chapter

THE LAST SEVERAL MONTHS HAVE GIVEN ME THE PRECIOUS GIFT OF time to reflect on my life and to decide how I would like to invest my remaining decades. I have experienced a significant transformation that has opened my eyes to the need to clearly observe and understand myself better. What started as a journey through cancer has evolved into a journey towards self-awareness. What started as a book about consulting has evolved into a book about the opportunity for an authentic transformation in the global consulting industry.

Coincidentally (although I don't believe in coincidences), my transformation and movement towards a more enlightened life has overlapped with massive transformations unfolding around the globe—with sudden shifts in awareness about racism and the citizenry finally hearing the anguished and frustrated cries for more inclusive and equitable approaches to our communities and nations.

We have been given an enormous opportunity to observe and learn from contrasts and extremes. Many of us, including privileged White people, are tired of the divisive, me-first, self-interested, and greed-filled approaches to life and to business.

I sense a strong shift is emerging in the way our communities will move forward. I am most familiar with the consulting world, and I chose to begin my focus on transformation in a familiar industry. I am seeking and acting on opportunities that will allow me to move forward in a more aware and authentic manner.

It seems now that the people who will be disadvantaged going forward are those who are either

- unaware of or unconscious to the massive shifts taking place; or
- privileged but without an understanding of how privilege needs to be translated into meaningful actions and outcomes.

As I noted earlier in this book, the consulting business is not complicated. It's essentially about five components:

- Understanding your market and services;
- Finding clients with work you can deliver;
- Delivering that work in a high-quality and effective manner;
- Making sure you get paid for that work; and
- Finding the next project to deliver.

Anyone can achieve success in a consulting firm; the degree of success, however, will depend upon your expertise. More importantly, it will hinge on your level of self-awareness and your ability to understand other people more fully (e.g., clients, colleagues, stakeholders).

I now better understand that our egos play a fundamental and sometimes destructive and distracting role in our personal and professional lives. Learning to observe your own ego and the egos around you will begin to allow you to better understand what's really happening in your workplace. We are all the same; we come from the same source, and we all have egos.

Those who are driven by egoic thinking are those who want to control and manipulate situations and people, at least in part to feel better about themselves. Fear drives the actions and reactions of many professionals: fear of failure, fear of falling behind their colleagues, fear of letting their supervisors down. In fact, the emotion underlying arrogance is often fear. Our egos take advantage of those fears and tend to push us towards negative thinking and emotions that will serve as individual and collective barriers to success.

Through several months of surgery and treatment to address a sudden diagnosis of an aggressive form of cancer, I was given a gift of time and space to reflect on my life. I was able to learn a great deal about myself, and I have been able to look back on a successful (by most standard measures) consulting career. Through meditation and deep reflection, I am also grateful to remember my true purpose; that is, to use my ecological and business knowledge, experience, and wisdom to inspire positive outlooks and outcomes.

My awakening has contributed to transforming how I work with people and how I communicate more effectively. Self-awareness provides a wonderful basis for a more joyful and intentional life and professional career. It also begins to open a door to the larger picture of life.

"Being truly aware means you are awake in the moment" (Gonzalez 2012). Our inner purpose is to awaken. Our outer purpose will change over time. Opening yourself to the emerging consciousness and bringing light into this world becomes the primary purpose of life (Tolle 2005). Working with egos that illustrate a lack of self-awareness may alert you to the need to carefully assess where you are in your own self-awareness journey and whether your role and place in your awareness journey is consistent with the level of awareness in your current workplace.

I believe that we are all here on purpose. We are meant to create and co-create better outcomes for all our planet's places and residents. Your purpose tends to be a larger picture, not the specific aspects of your role. Your job and its title are simply the avenue you have chosen to progress through life. Your ultimate satisfaction with your work here will not be driven by what title you achieve or how many physical things you amass. Rather, your happiness will relate to how you have created better outcomes. We are meant to awaken; that could include changing elements in our lives that serve as barriers to our happiness and fulfillment.

Is your current role in your company and industry being completed in a manner that is respectful, inclusive, creative, and helpful to people, communities, and nature? Or is your role dependent upon the shallower purposes of ego-driven interests such as greed, exploitation, and the capturing of controlling power? Those ego-driven elements are what most people seem to depend on and strive for. We are often so busy consuming that we can't or don't remember that we were given opportunities here to make better choices and to drive toward better results.

Most of us are asleep, and our real purpose here is to awaken to the broader and more positive reasons for our presence. Being more present allows you to immerse yourself in the activities of the moment. It doesn't allow you to dwell in the past or worry about the future. Or as a counsellor once put it to me, "If you keep one foot in the past and one foot in the future, you will piss all over the present."

Two individuals in Ontario have played key roles in my awakening and spiritual transformation. I am grateful to a life architect who has recently shifted to transformational healing, Kelly Benoit, for her guidance and wisdom over the years. I am also grateful to Sylvia Plester-Silk, a leadership coach and an Akashic record reader.

Thinking differently about consulting means being open to thinking differently about life. Traditional sources of guidance are helpful, but my awakening has been informed by these two individuals in particular. I have moved toward a new form of spiritual enlightenment that I could not have imagined before my cancer journey.

Awakening for you might simply mean that you want to shift your focus in consulting away from helping to maximize yields and profits to a position to generate more balanced outcomes. Are you and your company making a genuine difference?

It's important to consider these larger questions as you evaluate where you want to work and how you want to work. You could choose to improve the culture of your existing workplace by helping to awaken staff and the firm's leadership if they are receptive to change and to increasing their singular and collective self-awareness. Or perhaps you are at a place in your career where you are meant to seek out a more enlightened workplace or to start your own business to form and create the culture that you believe will generate better results.

Just because you may not want to be driven by egoic thinking, which is generally asleep to improving common outcomes, doesn't mean that you won't create profit and abundance. Through living a more positive life, you have an opportunity to attract more of what you desire. We all have the courage and love within us to make better choices.

In my case, my awakening has prompted me to step away from typical and traditional consulting models to create more enlightened firms. I have been given an opportunity to establish a family of companies under the name *Colucent*. These firms are meant to support the transformation of consulting and media businesses and to create authentic and positive social, environmental, and economic changes and outcomes.

The name Colucent was intentionally selected, not as a brand, but as a theme underlying this vision.

Lucent means glowing with light and marked by clarity. In this case, it means that Colucent enterprises will shine a positive and clarifying light on all of our endeavours. The word lucent was first recognized and used between 1490 and 1500, during the Renaissance, an intense period of European cultural, artistic, political, and economic rebirth following the Middle Ages. The Renaissance generated some of the world's greatest thinkers, authors, states-people, scientists, and artists. I'm emerging from my own personal rebirth inspired by a stem-cell transplant and recovery from a challenging cancer journey.

The prefix co emerged in English in the seventeenth century. It means together, mutually, in common. In my case, it means working together, sharing and recognizing what we have in common as a global society.

Colucent means operating in a transformational manner, always seeking new and better outcomes, while shining a bright light on a positive path forward. Colucent stands with the world's Indigenous peoples, their cultures, and their languages. It is a BIPOC-friendly group of companies, striving to embrace diversity and inclusion.

There are some basic principles that I have used to define the paths of these new ventures. I offer them in case they resonate with you and light up opportunities and specific examples of where you might take your consulting businesses.

1. **Integrity**

   We understand principles that reflect important ethics and values, and we practise them daily. And we know what right and wrong mean and that decisions that are made with integrity are not always the most convenient.

   To be specific, although we aren't yet large corporations in Canada, the Colucent family of companies accepts and actively endorses Call to Action 92 from the Truth and Reconciliation Commission of Canada's (2015) report. It reads: *"We call upon the corporate sector to adopt the United Nations Declaration on the Rights of Indigenous peoples as a guideline for reconciliation."* You don't have to be a large corporation to do the right thing.

2. **Wisdom**

   Over the course of our lives, we learn knowledge, gain experience, and become wise. Wisdom underlies the Colucent family of companies—it allows us to share and intelligently co-create meaningful outcomes.

3. **Exploration & Curiosity**

   We forge new paths. And we are excited by innovative ideas and approaches.

4. **Engagement**

   Colucent employs a collaborative approach focused on genuine and inclusive engagement, and we co-create and encourage positive messaging. We are open to and respect all races, religions, belief systems, cultures, ages, and genders, and we actively call out individuals and groups who discriminate. Colucent implements a respectful, living-wage internship program, and we work to decolonize the sectors that we work in, meaning that we actively support and act to divest our work and supporting materials and partners of the influence of colonial power and associated White privilege. We also support others actively decolonizing bureaucratic, cultural, linguistic, and psychological systems and communities.

5. **Generosity**

A spirit of generosity is a core part of our DNA. We believe in sharing and giving back—creating and distributing messaging and outcomes that will improve lives.

6. **Kindness**

Kindness is being friendly and considerate. Affection, gentleness, warmth, concern, and empathy are words associated with kindness. Being kind often requires courage and strength. All our ventures are rooted in kindness and authenticity.

I believe that the next leg in my career will be the most meaningful and fulfilling. I hope that something in this book might resonate with you and potentially help you embark on or continue your own personal and professional transformational journey. The consulting industry will be improved as more of us awaken to our true purpose, and as we operate genuinely in alignment with that purpose.

PART TWO

Chapter 11

What is the Consulting Industry Like Today?

NOW THAT WE HAVE SPOKEN TO AN UNDERSTANDING OF SELF-AWARE-ness and enlightenment, I want to share a few more ideas with you. Part Two provides additional thinking on the environmental consulting industry, including the types of projects and services that I have encountered over my career and the types of clients, stakeholders, and Indigenous peoples you might expect to work with.

I'm most familiar with the environmental consulting industry, which is now over 50 years old. In the United States alone, this business has grown to about US$30 billion in annual revenues. Orbis Research reports the US environmental consulting services market is estimated to reach US$43.8 billion by 2025 from US$29.7 billion in 2016.

The environmental sector remains relatively small, representing, for example, only about ten percent of the revenues achieved by the management consulting industry. North America and Europe have mature management consulting markets, with the largest management consulting firms being Accenture, Deloitte, and McKinsey & Company. In 2018, the global management consulting industry was valued around US$272 billion.

With over 57,000 businesses in the US environmental consulting market alone, it's challenging to discuss the specific nature of each of these firms.

There are, however, several broad, key differentiators amongst environmental consulting firms, the most apparent being size. Others include geographic diversity, services provided, and sectors served.

The largest consulting firms (or behemoths), which include environmental consulting as part of the services offered, include AECOM, Worley Parsons, Bechtel, Jacobs, Wood, SNC-Lavalin Group, AMEC Foster Wheeler, WSP, Arcadis, and Stantec. These larger firms are more formally structured with supporting bureaucracies and systems. They typically have larger overhead costs to accommodate those hierarchies. While the achievement of this larger scale of business can enable a firm to take on substantial, longer-term, and more complex assignments, this scale can also negatively affect an ability to move swiftly in response to rapidly emerging or changing markets, and to the strategic positioning of competitors. The moment we are in now with the raging COVID-19 pandemic and the emerging, rapid spread of the Omicron variant seems to be one of those periods of rapidly changing markets that may not favour behemoths.

The larger firms operate at a significant scale in terms of technical disciplines, geographic range, and total staff. In most cases, these firms are dominated by engineering and/or management services, with limited numbers of staff focused on the traditional and emerging environmental markets. Early in the industry's history, environmental services served as a loss leader for larger design and engineering projects. In some firms and cultures, that attitude has persisted. Loss leader refers to completing the early environmental work at no cost or at a reduced cost to the client in exchange for sole responsibility for downstream, traditionally more lucrative, design and construction consulting.

Over time, various engineering, planning, and management firms have added environmental experts in-house. In many cases, on larger assignments, despite their size, these larger firms need to harness and engage small and medium-sized environmental firms or talent pools to deliver on client expectations. Firms with preferred and consistent relationships with valued consultants can achieve more. Those relationships can take time to develop and benefit from ongoing, authentic engagement and the exchange of ideas (e.g., heads-up on assignments in the pipeline that might benefit from collaborative marketing; sharing of industry, regulatory, and technical knowledge).

Smaller to medium-sized firms (e.g., GHD, ICF International, Environmental Resources Management/ERM, Tetra Tech, Ausenco, SLR) compete for larger assignments or are drawn into alliances that could potentially win larger assignments. They depend upon mid-sized contracts to achieve the bulk of their revenue and profitability targets. This category of firms can be very successful, depending, of course, on the leadership and character of individual firms. They can adapt more rapidly than the behemoths, and they still have some ability to invest substantially in research and innovation.

Another category of environmental consulting firm, the niche or boutique operation, tends to be much smaller (e.g., fewer than 100 staff) and is more likely to be focused on a particular geography or service (traditional and/or emerging). These firms are generally able to move more quickly in the marketplace, and they may engage in a modest level of innovation (e.g., software development, scientific technology development and application).

Over the decades, these niche firms have tended to be targeted for acquisition by mid-sized and larger consultancies seeking to gain access to technologies, geographic areas, market sectors, and clients.

There are operational scenarios encountered that can affect a firm's size and growth trajectory. Starting at the smallest level, the sole proprietor of a one-person firm wears many hats. If that individual decides to grow the firm to around 12 staff, the firm begins to note that some better operational systems and some additional administrative staff are required to manage the small firm. Similar thresholds are reached at around 30, 60, and 120 staff.

As firms reach the mid-sized market, systems again become stretched, as do the administrative, accounting, legal, and human resource support capabilities. When led and managed well, these shortages can be handled with more strategic, selective, and lean approaches. Where they become unmanageable and present gaps or shortfalls, and where these aspects present new limits to growth, the positioning and sale of the mid-sized, slipping firms to larger, more efficient operations may be the more attractive alternative. This will especially be the case when early indicators point towards key staff looking for alternative places to work, or more dauntingly, to start their own competing firms.

Several books, resources, and associations provide guidance on how to engage in all aspects of traditional consulting (e.g., Gartner 2008; Balardo 2019; Maister 1993; Weiss 2011; D'Elia et al. 1984). Rather than repeating those basics, I have chosen to offer some observations and guidance as to what has worked better in my experience and what ongoing transformations in the industry will look like. Because of my experience in environmental consulting, most of my observations reflect that bias and knowledge base.

Chapter 12

Types of Environmental Consulting
Projects and Services

THE PRIMARY MARKETS FOR ENVIRONMENTAL SERVICES (AND MANY other services) include public and private clients. Most services are offered to the following client groups:

- Water Management

- Waste Management

- Mining

- Energy and Utilities

- Chemicals and Petroleum

- Manufacturing and Process Industries

- Land and Water Development (residential, commercial, industrial, institutional)

- Public and Public–Private Infrastructure (land development, energy facilities, ports, rail, roads, airports)

- Public Policy Development and Implementation

- Tourism and Ecotourism

- Indigenous Peoples Development

- ENGOs.

Identifying Clients and Their Characteristics

The various clients for environmental services have specific characteristics, and in some cases specific personalities. Understanding clients is a traditional and an essential ingredient in consulting. In the following subsections, I also offer some suggestions about where clients and markets are beginning to evolve or transform and where they will continue to operate.

Private-sector clients tend to be faster moving and are driven towards some level of approvals and permitting to develop facilities and processes. The private sector is affected by general economic indicators and by interest rates. Governments, while typically more bureaucratic, are slower moving and are dependent upon and reflective of local politics. Government agencies are also affected by economic indicators (e.g., availability of tax revenues).

Major client types are discussed further in the following sections.

Governments and Crown Corporations

Political systems vary around the world and include parliamentary republican systems (e.g., Iceland, Germany, Iraq, India), constitutional monarchies (e.g., Canada, Denmark, Japan, United Kingdom), presidential systems (e.g., United States, Afghanistan, Indonesia, Mexico), one-party states (e.g., China, Cuba, Vietnam), and military dictatorships (e.g., Sudan).

It's clear that governments are structured and operate very differently from country to country. Commonwealth countries appear to be similarly organized around three governance levels: federal, provincial/territory, and local.

Governments will retain consultants to support the planning and design of processes and services and the development of important infrastructure and public spaces. They may also retain consultants for the development of legislation, policies, and guidelines. Governments and associated agencies, commissions, and committees also employ firms for peer reviewing and contributing to the evaluation and testing of various applications from the private sector.

As governments become more constricted in terms of available budgets, I expect we will continue to see a shift towards the heavier use of third-party, peer-review services. This expanding market will become more significant, especially in jurisdictions with shrinking regulatory capacity. In some instances, peer-review exercises have become ineffective and inefficient as they turn into new, original work and studies, rather than simply providing professional review services.

Effective peer-review processes need to be clearly defined to prevent such challenges and obstacles in terms of the determination of key questions:

- Was the work conducted done so within the bounds of standard methods and protocols?
- Are the data sufficient to support the required analyses?
- Are the conclusions and recommendations fully supported by the work completed?

Peer-review work is not about gathering and assessing new and original data; it's about reviewing what others have done.

Higher-level governments typically oversee activities, projects, and land-use change over large areas, which may cross local government boundaries. Governments may retain consultants or consulting teams for planning over broad, cross-jurisdictional geographies, including watersheds, subwatersheds, coastal zones, and broad regional areas (e.g., Yellowstone to Yukon Conservation Initiative, Algonquin to Adirondacks Collaborative, Niagara and Onondaga Escarpments, Oak Ridges Moraine, Meso-American Conservation Corridor).

Governments principally perform planning and regulatory functions. Approaches can vary by jurisdiction. Regulators include those who review and respond to project applications and those who recommend or reject project approval. Local public works are characterized by the needs and desires of the local community. Projects that are delivered at a more local level often include public infrastructure such as roads, sewers, water-pollution control facilities, power facilities, and distribution networks.

Approaches on some public-sector projects are determined in part by political interests of various constituencies. The success of public projects depends upon the appropriate inclusion of all stakeholders and the management of the politics of a situation. Avoiding interference in various planning processes by misinformed and/or self-interested participants is important in maintaining the integrity of approvals processes.

Other challenges for working with government clients can include highly competitive bid requirements and relatively low thresholds for sole-source assignments, delays associated with the completion of agreements, and the timely payment of invoices. General project and program delays can negatively affect profitability, and procurement systems that promote holdbacks and milestone payments may generate challenges with consulting cash flow.

Associated with governments are various international institutions that have grown mostly from international conventions and agreements. Some of them will also serve as clients for consultants involved in more specialized areas; examples follow in the next two paragraphs.

At a global scale, the International Union for the Protection of Nature (1948–1956) was replaced in 1948 by the International Union for the Conservation of Nature (IUCN), an organization that continues to operate today. A 1973 conference in Washington, D.C., led 80 nations to sign the Convention on International Trade in Endangered Species of Wild Fauna and Flora (CITES). CITES monitors, and in some cases, restricts international commerce in plant and animal species believed to be harmed by trade.

There are many other international environmental agreements, some of which include the Antarctic Treaty (1959), Convention on Biodiversity (1992), RAMSAR Convention on Wetlands of International Importance, Especially as Waterfowl Habitat (1971), UN Convention on the Law of the Sea (1982), Framework Convention on Climate Change (1992), the Kyoto Protocol (1997), and the Paris Agreement (2015).

The most unusual public-sector project I was involved in was an integrated coastal zone planning and management assignment in China. I co-led a team of experts to complete some rapid coastal-zone assessments in Liaoning, Shandong, Jiangsu, and Fujian provinces. Our work was a prerequisite to the World Bank lending US$135 million to China to upgrade its coastal-zone management systems and infrastructure. We were treated like royalty, with at least one banquet each day.

I learned a lot about Chinese politics and business on my trips to Hong Kong and China. It was routine for our hotel phones to be listened to as we made calls to our government client. One afternoon, I found members of the Chinese delegation sleeping in our hotel rooms. The Chinese hosts sent women to our tables (dominated by men) after dinner in case we needed any company, something I found unfortunate and uncomfortable.

We were treated to the finest food and drink. I'm surprised my liver survived the endless toasts with Moutai, China's national liquor. We also learned partway through our trip that our Chinese hosts would drink water while we were plied with endless supplies of the clear, water-like Moutai. It was tradition and expected that we would take turns singing to the table after dinner. It was like a competition to see who could survive the most toasts and sing the most incredible songs. Our Canadian team paled in comparison to our hosts. They sang lovely ballads while most of our team refused to sing.

The Moutai gave me the illusion of courage to stand and sing the only "ballad" that came to my mind. My children were young at the time, and I entertained our Chinese hosts with a clumsy rendition of "'A' You're Adorable," a 1978 song by Sharon, Lois, and Bram, Canadian entertainers who focused on young children with their songs. I strongly suspect that was the only time that song has been sung at a Chinese banquet.

Private Sector

The private sector is dominated by those who invest in, finance, build, and create things (e.g., buildings, highways, railways, quarries, pipelines, ports, mines, energy facilities). These efforts may, with large-scale infrastructure, include private/public partnerships. In most cases, private companies will retain consultants to assist with risk assessment, valuation, approvals, permitting, and monitoring.

Private companies are responsible for responding to legislation, policies, and guidelines with appropriate technical studies. Typically, private industry does not have sufficient internal expertise to complete activities and reporting to support approvals processes. Nor are they able to independently offer unbiased opinions and advice that can come from a third party. While public-sector projects can be affected by politics, private-sector projects can be affected by political trends and ideologies and financial and other market expectations (e.g., social licence to operate).

Some of the most memorable clients I have worked with in this sector have distinct personalities, generally driven by the personalities and egos of the senior leadership. Some are driven by an interest in helping people and communities flourish, while others are driven more by self-interest and profit. More challenging clients tend to include those who insist on controlling all aspects of projects, including efforts to control the professional work and messaging of their consultants.

These clients typically focus on any potential bad news (e.g., presence of significant risks or features, including species at risk) and attempt to diminish the technical findings by dismissing potential negative effects as localized, insignificant, and fully mitigable. These clients tend to be more aggressive with their consultants, pushing to minimize uncertainty and their corporate risks. They can also be more aggressive with regulatory agencies, NGOs, and other stakeholders.

Aggressive and self-interested clients, driven by egoic thinking, can test a consultant's ability to stand firm in their approaches and conclusions and challenge their interest in continuing with a client relationship. These situations can necessitate difficult discussions with clients. In a small number of cases over forty years, I have stepped away from unpleasant client relationships (i.e., those that did not share my or my organization's ethics and values) or from assignments because I could not support a project's objectives and expected outcomes.

One challenging assignment was a proposed residential development in what I believed was a relict or old-growth forest along the shoreline of a large, southern Ontario lake. It was the oldest forest that I had observed during my forty-year career. The proposed high-end residences were laid out on lots that in some cases were fully forested. The oldest trees (sugar maple and American beech) were over 300 years old, and the forest was habitat to substantial populations of American ginseng (*Panax quinque-folius*), a plant considered to be endangered in Ontario. The developer wouldn't change their plan, and I chose to walk away.

In three other situations, I was conducting fieldwork on lands proposed for residential development—some or all the important natural features had been cleared in an effort by the clients to maximize housing yields. In one case, a headwater stream and wetland were completely removed, and the cleared lands looked like they had been professionally groomed and vacuumed to obscure any residual evidence of the significant features. In that obvious and flagrant violation of local laws, I chose to step away from the assignment. I understand that the clearing of those features triggered a strong regulatory response.

That example reminded me of a similar situation, years earlier, when a developer used blower fans to accelerate the burning of a forested area and to obscure the smoke from being visible to nearby residents. It was the sort of thing I'd expect to happen in less regulated situations, not in one of the most developed areas in Canada.

In the other situations, I helped the client face the consequences of their actions, which included feature replacement or compensatory ecological restoration. I'm not surprised that some unethical (and in some cases illegal) efforts are used by a few private-sector clients. In Ontario, some of the rules around what should be significant and protected have become distorted and exaggerated, resulting in some clients deciding to take desperate risk-avoidance measures rather than face what would seem to be lengthy and complex approvals processes.

I have fortunately encountered these situations quite rarely. There also seems, however, to be an ethical diversity amongst consultants—another firm seems always at the ready to step in and continue with tenuous relationships and assignments.

Some of the challenging situations commonly encountered with some private-sector clients are

- clients who want to reduce consulting costs by approving limited technical investigations (e.g., missing key ecological fieldwork windows where certain species and features might be more accurately defined or delineated, limiting subsurface examinations given cost impacts);

- efforts by clients to substantially edit conclusions and recommendations in the consultant's draft reporting (e.g., balking at proposed mitigation and monitoring measures that will increase and extend post-development costs); and

- efforts by clients to prevent their own experts from contacting and interacting transparently with regulatory agencies and other affected stakeholders.

In the private sector, much of the work is awarded based on relationships and on a non-competitive basis. When competitive bid situations are encountered, the lowest price tends to drive the selection of consultants. For clients who are less aware of or less familiar with approvals processes, this can set up a more difficult and complex approvals process. Some consulting firms will take advantage of a client's naiveté and leave out technical services with the intention to add them back as scope changes after contract award.

As technical gaps are identified as part of regulatory or third-party reviews, these gaps, which may have saved some short-term costs, may lead to significant delays in approvals processes (i.e., can extend a project for several months until these gaps are filled). The extension of approvals timeframes can create significant and unexpected costs to private-sector proponents. As the consulting industry transforms, those companies with strong ethics and a commitment to engaging the top experts in their field will withstand competitive pressures and will deliver more viable, risk-reducing outcomes for clients.

Indigenous Peoples

One of the more significant areas of market transformation for consulting is occurring in the Indigenous marketplace. Some of these markets are evolving and emerging as a substantial source of business for consultants, especially for Indigenous-owned firms. Indigenous markets are complex and can require significant learning investments and understanding from non-Indigenous consultants. It is rarely helpful to approach and engage with Indigenous peoples in a Western manner that includes a more typical egoic consulting attitude.

Respectful and truthful relationships are fundamental to successful engagement with Indigenous peoples. Those are not always a traditional consulting firm's *modus operandi*. This emerging market demands a more comprehensive explanation and specific considerations. It's fundamental to begin to develop a more fulsome understanding of who Indigenous peoples are and how history has shaped individuals, communities, and markets.

The United Nations Permanent Forum on Indigenous Issues notes that there are more than 370 million Indigenous people spread across seventy countries worldwide; that represents about five percent of the world's population. The UN Development Program reports between 370 and 500 million Indigenous peoples across ninety countries, representing 5,000 cultures. The UN supports self-identification; the term Indigenous has prevailed as a generic term for many years. In some countries, there may be preference for other terms, including tribes, first peoples, first nations, aboriginals, or ethnic groups.

The UN has issued the United Nations Declaration on the Rights of Indigenous Peoples (UNDRIP). I recommend reading it, if you haven't already. It affirms that *"indigenous peoples are equal to all other peoples, while recognizing the right of all peoples to be different, to consider themselves different, and to be respected as such...* It also affirms that *... all peoples contribute to the diversity and richness of civilizations and cultures, which constitute the common heritage of humankind...* and reaffirms that *... indigenous peoples, in the exercise of their rights, should be free from discrimination of any kind."*

The UNDRIP also recognizes the *"urgent need to respect and promote the inherent rights of indigenous peoples which derive from their political, economic, and social structures and from their cultures, spiritual traditions, histories, and philosophies, especially their rights to their lands, territories, and resources."*

Indigenous peoples are the holders of unique languages, knowledge systems, and beliefs and possess invaluable knowledge of practices for the sustainable management of natural resources. Indigenous knowledge is linked to the land. "There are particular landscapes, and biomes where ceremonies are held, certain stories recited, medicines properly gathered, and transfers of knowledge properly authenticated" (Kermoal & Altamirano-Jiménez 2016). Their ancestral lands have a fundamental importance for their collective physical and cultural survival as peoples. Indigenous peoples hold their own diverse concepts of development, based on their traditional values, visions, needs, and priorities (United Nations Permanent Forum on Indigenous Issues 2020).

Indigenous peoples have long suffered a variety of negative impacts, most of which are associated with colonialism, oppression, racism, and the introduction of fatal and debilitating diseases from other cultures (i.e., during colonialism). Colonialism by White Europeans has been a dominant and negatively impactful method employed in the expansion of European empires. Much has been written about the colonial oppression. One book that speaks to this topic, *Minik, The New York Eskimo* (Harper 2017) paints a picture of racism and early America's ignorance in the treatment of Indigenous people as specimens for public entertainment. I'm grateful to a friend in Iqaluit who sent me this book; it's one of the pieces I frequently look back to while I continue my own personal reconciliation journey.

I have learned quite a bit about the impacts of colonization on global Indigenous peoples through continuing education (e.g., University of Alberta, Indigenous Canada course), not through my earlier formal education. The absence of the truths of how Canada was developed has resulted in an easier perpetuation of White privilege and blissful ignorance of the genocide of Indigenous peoples underlying the founding of many nations, including Canada.

It's clear that non-Indigenous people have oppressed Indigenous peoples around the world under many banners, including empire building. As I have become more self-aware, I have opened my eyes to my kinship with all peoples, including Indigenous peoples. I now see that we are, at our core, essentially the same; when we step away from our egoic patterns of thought, we can get a glimpse of how much we share in common.

I have become saddened by what I have learned about the historic and ongoing oppression of Indigenous peoples around the world. Most recently, oppression continues in the form of illegal and immoral assaults on Indigenous communities for legal and illegal agriculture, mining, and forestry operations (e.g., Arariboia peoples on Amazonian Indigenous lands).

It's quite clear that egoic thinking plays a significant role in this ongoing oppression. Many privileged people automatically assume they are better than Indigenous peoples or other members of the BIPOC community. It's this reflex belief that negates authentic and transformative progress.

I have observed that belief in person, while negotiating on behalf of three Ontario First Nations to achieve the environmental approvals required to build a 300-megawatt renewable energy windfarm. I witnessed consultants, contractors, and senior government officials making or implying disparaging remarks and attitudes about my clients and about Indigenous peoples more generally. Some Western, non-Indigenous professionals identified themselves as Indigenous experts. They seemed ill informed and quite dismissive of the ability of the Indigenous peoples to understand their land in the way Western science could. That's ironic given that the Indigenous peoples have lived on and with these lands for millennia. The Western scientists involved in the environmental approvals work only visited those lands periodically over a couple of years.

Geniusz (2009) is one of many Indigenous peoples working to decolonize all aspects of Indigenous lives. She provides an interesting perspective on the colonization, driven in part by the European pursuit of botanical information and knowledge (e.g., traditional medicines). She directly addresses the need for the decolonization of early books and articles created by colonizers who did not understand the Anishinaabe people (who lived across the Great Lakes into the western plains in what is now referred to as Canada and the United States) and their traditional knowledge and wisdom. Interestingly, a less than fully transparent bioprospecting industry persists to this day, devoted to the exploitation and patenting of native plant and animal species.

All perspectives need to be considered and included in the Indigenous movements towards reconciliation and justice. For consultants (and for society in general), it's important to acknowledge, accept, and respect that justice is an appropriate demand, when people, communities, and populations have not been treated fairly or have been treated dishonestly and inequitably. Many governments, institutions, powerful and influential groups, and business interests, and even members of some NGOs, have been involved in negative and destructive practices against Indigenous peoples (intentionally and unintentionally).

Canada, like many nations, has a long history of oppression of, and discrimination against, Indigenous peoples. Almost 1.7 million people in Canada's population of about 37 million identify as being Indigenous. Indigenous peoples represent 630 First Nations in Canada and reside throughout the country in urban and rural areas. Many occupy about 3,000 reserves. Canada's Truth and Reconciliation Commission completed an extensive six-year process and issued its final report, *Honouring the Truth, Reconciling for the Future,* in 2015. Created from the Indian

Residential Schools Settlement Agreement, it opens the door for truth and reconciliation.

On February 14, 2018, Prime Minister Justin Trudeau, announced that the Government of Canada *"will fundamentally transform the relationships with Indigenous peoples by basing the relationship on the recognition and implementation of Indigenous rights."*

Before consultants engage with Indigenous peoples, nations, and communities, the following actions are recommended. Most are drawn from Joseph and Joseph (2019):

- Read and understand the history of the treatment of Indigenous peoples by colonizers and their governments;
- Understand common threads in Indigenous worldviews;
- Learn about the history, worldview, culture, values, and traditions of each community that you work with;
- Learn about and understand the issues and barriers to employment faced by Indigenous peoples; and
- Understand and respect the shift towards decolonization, self-determination, self-reliance, and self-government amongst Indigenous peoples.

Consulting with and on behalf of Indigenous peoples requires a greater depth of understanding, dialogue, and relationship building than traditional, non-Indigenous projects and clients. It also demands, as Banaji and Greenwald (2013) noted, a self-assessment of our own biases, hidden and overt (e.g., biases based on gender, race, religion, age, nationality, occupation).

Environmental Non-governmental Organizations (ENGOs)

ENGOs include various business models and represent a range of perspectives; it's a complex group that in some cases has experienced controversy.

ENGOs began to emerge around the 1900s (e.g., Wildlife Conservation Society, 1895; The Nature Conservancy, 1915; Western Australia Naturalists' Club, 1924; Nature Canada, 1939; World Wildlife Fund, 1961; Greenpeace, 1971). In some cases, these organizations grew around specific and local interests; others grew from a growing concern about the magnitude of environmental issues affecting our planet.

ENGOs may retain environmental consultants but the tendency in the ENGO industry is to focus investments and operating costs on various areas or thematic-based campaigns. Volunteers and citizen science play important roles in these groups and businesses. Greenpeace International, for example, claims support from 15,000 volunteers.

Each ENGO has its own personality; some have grown into substantial environmental businesses (e.g., Greenpeace, World Wildlife Fund, Conservation International). The World Wildlife Fund, established sixty years ago, has a presence in more than 100 countries, has one million members, and 2018 operating revenues of more than US$335 million. Greenpeace, formed in 1971, has a presence in fifty-five countries with 2018 revenues over €80 million. Conservation International, formed in 1915, had 2018 revenues of US$83 million, and Natural Resources Defense Council Inc. had 2018 annual revenues of more than US$190 million.

There are several medium to smaller-sized ENGOs, including Fauna and Flora International with 2018 income of over £19 million, and

Wetlands International with a 2018 income of over €8 million. The Earth Island Institute had 2017 total revenues of over US$14 million and the Environmental Defense Fund had 2018 total revenues of almost US$7 million.

Interestingly, ENGOs are also being affected by politics and by a reorganization of funding (e.g., the United States, Mexico). Environmental Defense Fund (2017) reports that *"the early months of the Trump administration saw a moment of genuine rebirth for the political salience of environmental issues—and a historic upwelling of support for our efforts. Hundreds of thousands took to the streets of Washington in the name of climate action and sound science. Donations to EDF and other organizations have set records. Polls show President Trump's environmental agenda is deeply unpopular."*

The Earth Island Institute reports that Mexican President Andrés Manuel López Obrador *"ran his left-wing campaign on the promise that he would expand social programs to help the vulnerable. He won in a landslide and took office in December 2018. In February 2019, however, he declared that the government would no longer fund NGOs"* (Jensen 2020).

A review of a range of representative ENGOs suggests that there are some shared purposes and some differentiating characteristics. Some seem to be strongly dependent upon the best available science to support decision-making and investments (e.g., Nature Conservancy of Canada). Other ENGOs seem to depend upon the use of exaggeration, negative and dramatic headlines, and associated negative stories (stoking fear and anger) to excite and ramp up revenues (i.e., membership growth and donations). It reminds me in some cases of the fake news narrative that started in the United States in 2016 and has been continuing and expanding worldwide (e.g., China, Brazil, France).

Examples of more negative or exaggerated messaging from ENGOs in my geographic area include statements such as the following:

- *Ontario government resumed their attack on farms, sustainable cities, nature, and affordable healthy living in the Greater Golden Horseshoe*
- *Secret memo reveals oil industry plan to exploit COVID crisis, endanger Canadians*
- *Don't let Ontario be gifted to developers!*
- *Help stop Ontario from bulldozing Nature!*
- *What's Next After Gutting Conservation Authorities?*
- *Countdown to destruction for these titanic turtles*
- *Government Runs Roughshod Over Environmental Protection and Democracy*
- *The oil industry wants to derail modernization of Canada's pollution law*
- *Steamrolling the way for development, behind closed doors*

It's also interesting to observe some ENGOs piling onto the Black Lives Matter anti-racism campaigns and the COVID-19 recovery, while overtly asking for donations to support a "just recovery." I've looked briefly at many of the North American ENGOs and note that most staff and boards seem to be dominated by White people. There is a growing understanding of the role of White privilege in some ENGOs and other organizations and institutions.

As with consultants, each ENGO has a reputation and degree of credibility based upon its history and accomplishments. Sometimes the language and messaging used in websites and campaigns can help to reveal an ENGO's culture and strategy.

Many of these ENGOs have become substantial environmental businesses, and a degree of controversy exists around potential conflicts of interest and the investments of monies received by some ENGOs. Bevington (2009) provides an interesting outline of the history of the environmental conservation movement in the United States and three paths to biodiversity protection: national environmental organizations, Earth-first, and grassroots biodiversity groups. His book describes the role of various techniques and campaigns in the movements, such as political lobbying, insiders, and monkeywrenching, which have partially defined aspects of environmental activism. He speaks to the rise of grassroots biodiversity activism and the rebirth of environmental activism.

Mbaria and Ogada (2016) speak clearly about the role of some ENGOs in Kenya. They clearly present their thoughts about the role that conflicting needs, weak policies, consumption, and greed have played in blocking the opportunity for positive and meaningful wildlife conservation outcomes in Kenya.

There are also many other organizations, referred to as civil society organizations (CSOs), which include NGOs and ENGOs. The UN identifies civil society as the third sector of society, along with government and business. It comprises CSOs and NGOs. There are many CSOs; examples of these diverse groups include Caribbean Conference of Churches, Center for Economic and Social Rights, Earthstewards Network, and the International Fellowship of Reconciliation. The UN has a list of CSOs that may be helpful for consultants to determine whether some might be interested in various assignments, perspectives, and/or collaborative efforts.

Key Points and Observations:

PART TWO

1. Challenges and opportunities abound with all different kinds of consulting firms.

2. The largest consulting firms (or behemoths) are more formally structured with supporting bureaucracies and systems. They can take on substantial, longer-term, and more complex assignments, but they tend to move more slowly and with difficultly when responding to rapid market shifts.

3. Smaller to medium-sized firms depend upon mid-sized contracts to achieve the bulk of their revenue and profitability targets. This category of firms can be very successful, depending, of course, on the leadership and character of individual firms. They can adapt more rapidly than the behemoths, and they still have some ability to invest substantially in research and innovation.

4. Smaller niche or boutique operations are more focused on a particular geography or service. They can move more quickly in the marketplace, and they may engage in a modest level of innovation.

5. While they can be substantial sources of consulting projects, governments can also be quite challenging to work with given highly competitive bid requirements, relatively low thresholds for sole source assignments, delays associated with the completion of agreements, and the timely payment of invoices. These aspects can depress the profitability of consulting projects and firms.

6. Limit your Moutai consumption at banquets and memorize some intelligent and meaningful song lyrics, just in case.

7. Private-sector projects tend to be awarded more often based on relationships and on a non-competitive basis. Private assignments present opportunities for more rapid and meaningful results, but they can also be heavily affected by cumbersome regulatory environments.

8. Indigenous markets are evolving and emerging as a substantial source of business for consultants, especially for Indigenous-owned firms. Indigenous markets are complex and can require substantial learning investments and understanding from non-Indigenous consultants. It is rarely helpful to approach and engage with Indigenous peoples in a Western manner with a more typical egoic consulting attitude.

Afterword

I BEGAN WRITING THIS AFTERWORD ON JANUARY 6, 2021, A DAY OF infamy in American history. I spent most of that day in transit, returning home from a trip to Victoria, British Columbia, where I helped our son set up for a co-op work-term. Since recovering from cancer, everything feels brand new. I've always felt young and playful, but the opportunity to fly again, the first time in about 18 months, felt wondrous—despite all of the necessary precautions due to COVID-19. I was glued to the cabin window, snapping pictures of the coastal mountains, the interior of British Columbia, the Rockies, the foothills, the prairies, and the forests and wetlands of northern Minnesota. From forty-thousand feet above North America, everything looked calm and serene. Little did I know that the scene at the Capitol Building in Washington, D.C., was anything but calm and serene. An attempted insurrection was underway.

It was the day an ego-driven political regime escalated its descent from power. In his Save America Rally, former President Trump's choppy, redundant, and misinformed rhetoric helped to inspire a mob to move toward and breach the American Capitol Building. The mob caused significant physical and psychological damage, and sadly, the loss of lives.

The events that have transpired since January 6 present a clear, albeit extreme, example of how a lack of self-awareness and egoic thinking, a core theme in this book, can deepen negative outcomes.

The stark contrast in political and human beliefs that has been heightened since January 6 is stunning. Contrast can serve as a helpful teacher—showing us more clearly what we want and don't want. In this case, the contrast has allowed a growing number of people to choose truth, authenticity, and the equitable treatment of all people over misinformed and ignorant reactions.

Contrast can also serve as an inspiration to move people and communities towards a deeper understanding of true character, emotions, motives, and desires. The same can be said for countries, cities, and communities; they are no better or worse than others. We are essentially the same. Collectively we need to become much more aware of the importance of equality and inclusivity.

In consulting and in life, I believe that we are meant to support one another and to respect our differences. In consulting companies that believe that they are better than their competitors, those attitudes and behaviours generally come from a place of fear and egoic thinking—fundamentally flowing from a lack of self-awareness.

As I have thought more deeply about my life journey, I can see where my choices have been unwise at times, and I can more clearly see where my choices have not always contributed to better outcomes. I can look at my path with a new level of self-awareness and a new level of self-forgiveness. And I can respect and forgive those I am connected to when their choices seem at odds with positive outcomes. I can see where authenticity exists and where people seem to be stuck in a place of egoic thinking with an absence or complete lack of self-awareness. And that's okay. I have moved away from judging others as harshly as I have in the past.

I now understand that we can live together with our differences and that we are not here to fight against one another. Rather, we are here to help each other discover our humanness and to support each other, regardless of cultural, religious, spiritual, race, gender, and political beliefs or other differences.

My consulting work is coming into alignment with who I truly am. After 40 years in the consulting industry, I'm adjusting my course. I am creating firms that are based on authentic relationships with everyone I interact with. In recent months, I have begun to engage with my network in much more meaningful ways. Every project I undertake is designed to produce better outcomes. I am not only thinking outside the box, I'm thinking without boxes and without the constraints of traditional consulting thinking and approaches.

I'm working on purpose and am dedicating much of my time and energy to bridging often-polarized positions, and I'm actively engaging with people in what have been labelled BIPOC communities. I'm not generally a fan of labels, but I use that acronym because it seems to be well accepted and helps recognize more marginalized and disrespected individuals and communities. My new ventures are strongly rooted in helping to create more equitable and inclusive outcomes. I have decided to focus my remaining decades of work and play on disrupting inauthenticity.

I hope that readers will find this book interesting and helpful. It has been a journey for me to write—a journey that has intertwined with reflections on my personal and professional life. Moving into my fifth decade of consulting, I feel inspired and unstoppable. This book has allowed me to see and understand my purpose more clearly.

I am deeply grateful for the opportunity to continue my work, and I am grateful for the contrasts that I have been able to experience and observe. The gifts of cancer and time to pause and reflect have contributed significantly to my own enlightenment.

References and Helpful, Inspiring Resources

Aikenhead, Glen, and Herman Michell. *Bridging Cultures: Indigenous and Scientific Ways of Knowing Nature*. Toronto: Pearson Canada, 2011.

Armstrong, Sally. *Power Shift: The Longest Revolution*. Toronto: House of Anansi Press, 2019.

Balardo, Wayne. *Genetics of Independent Consulting: Lessons Learned Over 30 Years*. Middletown, DE: Zoedie, 2019.

Banaji, Mahzarin R., and Anthony Greenwald. *Blindspot: Hidden Biases of Good People*. New York: Bantam Books, 2013.

Barton, Hugh. *City of Well-being. A Radical Guide to Planning*. New York: Routledge, 2017.

Bevington, Douglas. *The Rebirth of Environmentalism: Grassroots Activism from the Spotted Owl to the Polar Bear*. Washington, DC: Island Press, 2009.

Bradberry, Travis, and Jean Greaves. *Emotional Intelligence 2.0*. San Diego: Talentsmart, 2009.

Brady, Chris, and Orrin Woodward. *Life Leadership*. Cary, NC: Obstaclés Press, 2013.

Brown, Brené. *Daring Greatly: How the Courage to Be Vulnerable Transforms the Way We Live, Love, Parent and Lead*. New York: Avery, 2012.

Brown, Valerie A., John A. Harris, and Jacqueline Y. Russell, eds. *Tackling Wicked Problems: Through the Transdisciplinary Imagination*. London, England: Earthscan, 2010.

Business Research Company. *Environmental Consulting Services Global Market Opportunities and Strategies to 2021*. City: The Business Research Company, 2018. https://www.reportlinker.com/p05482365/ Environmental-Consulting-Services-Global-Market-Opportunities-And-Strategies-To.html.

Buzzell, Linda, and Craig Chalquist. *Ecotherapy: Healing with Nature in Mind*. Berkeley: Counterpoint, 2009.

Chugh, Dolly. *The Person You Mean to Be: How Good People Fight Bias*. Harper Business, 2018.

Connop, Stuart. "Nature-based solution evaluator indicators: *Environmental Indicators Review*." *Connecting Nature. Accessed September 13, 2021*. https:// connectingnature.eu/nature-based-solution-evaluation-indicators-environmental-indicators-review.

Corry, Stephen. *Tribal Peoples for Tomorrow's World*. London: Freeman Press, 2011.

Dalai Lama. *Beyond Religion: Ethics for a Whole World*. New York: First Mariner Books, 2012.

D'Elia, Sandy, Jim Ricereto, and Margaret Spaulding. *The A/E Marketing Handbook: A User's Manual*. Newington, CT: A/E Marketing Journal, 1984.

Dispenza, Joe. *Breaking the Habit of Being Yourself: How to Lose Your Mind and Create a New One*. Carlsbad, CA: Hay House, 2012.

Dyer, Judy. *The Highly Sensitive: How to Stop Emotional Overload, Relieve Anxiety, and Eliminate Negative Energy*. Bolton, ON: Pristine Publishing, 2018.

Dyer, Wayne. *Inspiration: Your Ultimate Calling*. Carlsbad, CA: Hay House, 2006.

Dyer, Wayne. *Wishes Fulfilled: Mastering the Art of Manifesting*. Carlsbad, CA: Hay House, 2012.

Edwards, Andres R. *The Sustainability Revolution: Portrait of a Paradigm Shift*. Gabriola Island, BC: New Society Publishers, 2005.

Environmental Defense Fund. "Pathways 2025." EDF *Strategic Plan*, 2017.

G., Akemi. *Why We Are Born: Remembering Our Purpose Through Akashic Records*. Coppell, TX: Self Published, 2014.

Gartner, John F. *Confessions of a Consultant*. Belleville, ON: Epic Press, 2008.

Geniusz, Wendy Makoons. *Our Knowledge Is Not Primitive: Decolonizing Botanical Anishinaabe Teachings*. Syracuse, NY: Syracuse University Press, 2009.

Gobster, Paul, H., and R. Bruce Hull. *Restoring Nature: Perspectives from the Social Sciences and Humanities*. Washington, DC: Island Press, 2000.

Gonzalez, Maria. Mindful Leadership: *The 9 Ways to Self-Awareness, Transforming Yourself and Inspiring Others*. Mississauga, ON: John Wiley & Sons Canada, 2012.

Gough, Ian. *Heat, Greed and Human Need: Climate Change, Capitalism and Sustainable Wellbeing*. Cheltenham, UK: Edward Elgar, 2017.

Hams, Brad. *Ownership Thinking: How to End Entitlement and Create a Culture of Accountability, Purpose, and Profit*. Toronto: McGraw-Hill, 2012.

Harnish, Verne. *Scaling Up: How a Few Companies Make It and Why the Rest Don't*. Ashburn, VA: Gazelles, 2014.

Harper, Kevin. *Minik, The New York Eskimo*. Hanover, NH: Steerforth Press, 2017.

Hawkins, David R. *Power vs. Force: The Hidden Determinants of Human Behaviour*. Carlsbad, CA: Hay House, 2002.

Helmer, Jodi. *Protecting Pollinators: How to Save the Creatures that Feed Our World*. Washington, DC: Island Press, 2019.

Hicks, Esther, and Jerry, Hicks. *Ask and It Is Given: Learning to Manifest Your Desires*. New York: Hay House, 2004.

Hicks, Esther, and Jerry Hicks. *The Astonishing Power of Emotions: Let Your Feelings Be Your Guide*. New York: Hay House, 2007.

Hicks, Esther, and Jerry Hicks. *The Vortex: Where the Law of Attraction Assembles All Cooperative Relationships*. New York: Hay House, 2009.

Intergovernmental Panel on Climate Change. *Climate Change and Land: Summary for Policy Makers*, 2020. https://www.ipcc.ch/site/assets/uploads/sites/4/2020/02/SPM_Updated-Jan20.pdf.

International Institute for Environment and Development. *IIED Strategy 2019–2024.* 2019. https://pubs.iied.org/17703iied.

Jarvis, Chase. *Creative Calling: Establish a Daily Practice, Infuse Your World with Meaning, and Succeed in Work + Life.* New York: Harper Business, 2019.

Jeffrey, Scott, ed. *Dissolving the Ego, Realizing the Self: Contemplations from the Teachings of David R. Hawkins.* Carlsbad, CA: Hay House, 2018.

Jensen, Sally. "Mexican NGOs Continue to Struggle with Federal Funding Cuts." *Earth Island Institute, February 6, 2020.* https://www.earthisland.org/journal/index.php/articles/entry/mexico-ngos-funding-lopez-obrador.

Jones, Michael. *Artful Leadership: Awakening the Commons of the Imagination.* Victoria, CA: Pianoscapes, 2006.

Joseph, Bob. *21 Things You May Not Know About the Indian Act: Helping Canadians Make Reconciliation with Indigenous Peoples a Reality.* Port Coquitlam, BC: Indigenous Relations Press, 2018.

Joseph, Bob, and Cynthia F. Joseph. *Indigenous Relations: Insights, Tips and Suggestions to Make Reconciliation a Reality.* Port Coquitlam, BC: Indigenous Relations Press, 2019.

Kienle, Peter, 2019. Why You Should Turn Your Does Into Sellers. Blog Post in PSMJ Resources Inc on 08/12/19. https://go.psmj.com/blog/why-you-should-turn-your-doers-into-sellers

Kermoal, Nathalie, and Isabel Altamirano-Jiménez. *Living on the Land: Indigenous Women's Understanding of Place.* Athabasca, AB: Athabasca University Press, 2016.

King, Andrew, Ben Henley, and David Hawkins. "What Is Pre-industrial Climate and Why Does It Matter?" *The Conversation,* June 7, 2017. https://theconversation.com/what-is-a-pre-industrial-climate-and-why-does-it-matter-78601.

Lakhiani, Vishen. *The Code of the Extraordinary Mind.* New York: Rodale, 2016.

Lovejoy, Thomas E., and Lee Hannah, eds. *Biodiversity and Climate Change: Transforming the Biosphere.* Newhaven, CT: Yale University Press, 2019.

Maister, David H. *Managing the Professional Service Firm.* New York: Free Press Paperbacks, 1993.

Mbaria, John, and Mordecai Ogada. *The Big Conservation Lie: The Untold Story of Wildlife Conservation in Kenya.* Auburn, WA: Lens&Pens Publishing, 2016.

McIntosh, Gary L., and Samuel D. Rima, Sr. *Overcoming the Dark Side of Leadership: The Paradox of Personal Dysfunction.* Grand Rapids, MI: Baker Books, 1997.

Meurisse, Thibault. *Master Your Emotions: A Practical Guide to Overcome Negativity and Better Manage Your Feelings.* San Bernardino, CA, 2019.

Moulden, Julia. *We Are the New Radicals: A Manifesto for Reinventing Yourself and Saving the World.* New York: The McGraw Hill Companies, 2018.

Pinsky, Denis. "Eleven Design and Development Best Practices for 2018." *Forbes,* February 12, 2018. https://www.forbes.com/sites/denispinsky/2018/02/12/website-design-standards/#11d46dc7f54f.

Robinson, Nicholas A., and Christian Walzer. "How Do We Prevent the Next Outbreak?" *Scientific American,* March 25, 2020. https://blogs.scientificamerican.com/observations/how-do-we-prevent-the-next-outbreak/.

Roman, Sanaya. *Personal Power Through Awareness: A Guidebook for Sensitive People.* Tiburon, CA: H. J. Kramer, 1986.

Roman, Sanaya. *Spiritual Growth: Being Your Higher Self.* Tiburon, CA: H. J. Kramer, 1989.

Ruiz, Don Miguel, and Don Jose Ruiz. *The Fifth Agreement: A Practical Guide to Self-Mastery.* San Rafael, CA: Amber-Allen, 2010.

Schein, Edgar H. *Humble Consulting: How to Provide Real Help Faster.* Oakland, CA: Berrett Koehler, 2016.

Selhub, Eva M., and Alan C. Logan. *Your Brain on Nature: The Science of Nature's Influence on Your Health, Happiness and Vitality.* Toronto: Collins, 2012.

Seppala, Emma. *The Happiness Track: How to Apply the Science of Happiness to Accelerate Your Success.* New York: Harper One, 2016.

Singer, Michael A. *The Untethered Soul: The Journey Beyond Yourself.* Oakland, CA: New Harbinger, 2007.

Steiner, Frederick. *Human Ecology: How Nature and Culture Shape Our World.* Washington, DC: Island Press, 2016.

Sullivan, Dan, and Gordon Allen. *The Advisor Century: Value Creation in an Entrepreneurial Society.* Toronto: The Strategic Coach, 2007.

Tamashiro, Tim. *How to Ikigai: Lessons for Finding Happiness and Living Your Life's Purpose.* Coral Gables, FL: Mango Publishing Group, 2019.

Think Boundless. *The Failed Promise of Freelance Consulting Talent Platforms.* 2020. https://think-boundless.com/the-failed-promise-of-freelance-consulting-talent-platforms/.

Tolle, Eckhart. *A New Earth, Awakening to Your Life's Purpose.* New York: Plume, 2005.

Tolle, Eckhart. *Transcending the Ego: Finding Our Roots in Being,* 2011. Audiobook, Read by Eckhart Tolle, 1 hour, 17 minutes.

Truth and Reconciliation Commission of Canada. *Calls to Action, Business and Reconciliation. Action 92.* 2015. https://www.rcaanc-cirnac.gc.ca/eng/1524506030545/1557513309443

Truth and Reconciliation Commission of Canada. *Final Report of the Truth and Reconciliation Commission of Canada, Volume One: Summary: Honouring the Truth and Reconciling for the Future,* Toronto: James Lorimer & Company, 2015.

Truth and Reconciliation Commission of Canada. *What We Have Learned: Principles of Truth and Reconciliation,* 2015. http://www.trc.ca/assets/pdf/Principles%20of%20Truth%20and%20Reconciliation.pdf.

United Nations. *Accredited Global Civil Society partners,* 2020. https://www.un.org/unispal/data-collection/ civil-society/list-of-intl-civil-society-partners/ international-civil-society-organizations-accredited-to-the-committee/.

United Nations. Civil Society webpage, 2020. https://www.un.org/en/sections/resources-different-audiences/civil-society/index.html.

United Nations Development Program. *10 Things to Know About Indigenous Peoples.* January 25, 2019.

United Nations Framework Convention on Climate Change. *What Do Adaptation to Climate Change and Climate Resilience Mean?* 2020. https:// unfccc.int/topics/adaptation-and-resilience/the-big-picture/ what-do-adaptation-to-climate-change-and-climate-resilience-mean

United Nations Permanent Forum on Indigenous Issues, 2020. *Who Are Indigenous Peoples, Factsheet.* https://www.un.org/esa/socdev/unpfii/ documents/5session_factsheet1.pdf

United States Geological Survey. Water Sciences School, *Environmental DNA (eDNA).* 2020. https://www.usgs.gov/special-topic/water-science-school/science/environmental-dna-edna?qt-science_center_objects=0#qt-science_center_objects.

Vanclay, Frank. *Social Impact Assessment: Guidance for assessing and managing the social impacts of projects.* Groningen, The Netherlands: University of Groningen, 2015.

Vaughan-Lee, Llewellyn, ed. *Spiritual Ecology: The Cry of the Earth.* Point Reyes, CA: The Golden Sufi Center, 2017.

Ward, Marguerite, and Melissa Wiley. "14 racist brands, mascots, and logos that were considered just another part of American life." *Business Insider,* June 23, 2020. https://www.businessinsider. com/15-racist-brand-mascots-and-logos-2014-6.

Weiss, Alan. *The Consulting Bible: Everything You Need to Know to Create and Expand a Seven Figure Consulting Practice.* Hoboken, NJ: John Wiley & Sons, 2011.

Williams, Florence. *The Nature Fix: Why Nature Makes Us Happier, Healthier and More Creative*. New York: W.W. Norton, 2017.

Wilson, Edward O. *In Search of Nature*. Washington, DC: Island Press/ Shearwater Books, 1996.

Woods, Kerri. *Human Rights and Environmental Sustainability*. Cheltenham, UK: Edward Elgar, 2010.

World Commission on Environment and Development. Our Common Future. Oxford: Oxford University Press, 1987.

Younging, Gregory. *Elements of Indigenous Style. A Guide for Writing By and About Indigenous Peoples*. Edmonton, AB: Brush Education, 2018.

Zimring, Carl A. *Clean and White: A History of Environmental Racism in the United States*. New York: New York University Press, 2015.

Appendix

Example Standard Terms and Conditions

---

1. Scope of Work

The Client has read, understood and agrees with the scope, schedule and pricing detailed in the Project Initiation/ Authorization Agreement and in any additional appended scope and methods materials.

Modifications to the agreed-upon scope are to be agreed upon in writing prior to the completion of additional work.

---

2. Conduct of the Work

Savanta Inc. will provide services in a timely manner under this agreement with the degree of care, skill and diligence normally provided in the performance of services, in respect of projects of a similar nature.

---

3. Record Keeping

As background technical materials may become part of reporting and/or evidence before tribunals, notes, field forms, photographs and associated technical materials will be created, organized and maintained in a careful, professional, and secure manner.

---

4. Health and Safety

Savanta abides by our internal, corporate Health and Safety Protocols.

5. Fees and Billing and Payment Procedures

Savanta will bill the client monthly for work completed, as per the following terms:

- The client will receive an invoice each month for services and reimbursable expenses charged/ incurred by Savanta Inc., during the previous month;
- Invoices are due upon receipt with cheques made payable to Savanta Inc.;
- Accounts requiring invoices to be split across clients, will be subject to a split management fee;
- Accounts outstanding for more than 60 days from date of issue will immediately be subject to interest at a rate of 2% per month;
- Where accounts are outstanding for more that 90 days, project work may be suspended until the accounts are cleared; and
- Where accounts that are outstanding for more than 90 days, are subject to invoice splits across clients, all project work may be suspended until the split invoices are cleared across all participating clients.

6. Indemnification

The Client shall indemnify and save harmless Savanta Inc., its employees, officers or agents, from and against all claims, actions, losses, expenses costs or damages of every nature and kind whatsoever in the performance of this agreement.

7. Confidentiality

Information collected, analyzed, and reported upon during work addressed by this agreement, shall not be used or divulged by Savanta Inc., their agents or employees without prior written approval of the Client.

This agreement shall not prohibit Savanta from acting to report or correct a situation for which they are compelled to do so by professional/legal obligations. If such a situation arises, Savanta Inc. shall immediately inform the Client of the requirement to do so.

About the Author

OVER THE PAST FOUR DECADES, TOM HAS FOCUSED HIS ENVIRONMEN-
tal consulting career on impact assessment, mitigation planning and
design, and ecological planning and restoration. He has been privileged to
lead hundreds of environmental assignments, including coastal zone and
regional landscape planning projects, major resource and infrastructure
project impact assessments (e.g., mineral aggregate quarries, landfills,
toxic waste disposal facilities, nuclear and renewable energy projects),
and urbanization studies. Tom has developed extensive tribunal experience, providing expert testimony on dozens of occasions.

Tom has inspired and led teams ranging from 35 to 250 members. In
2006, he created his own company, Savanta Inc., an entrepreneurial
enterprise focused on working collaboratively to create more positive and
meaningful outcomes. In early 2019, Tom sold Savanta and entered into
a life-changing process fuelled by the diagnosis, treatment, and recovery
from a rare and aggressive cancer. The gift of cancer gave Tom time to
reflect on life and his forty years in the consulting industry, and time to
write this book. He has been inspired through his successful recovery to
embark on the next chapter of his life—creating and leading some emerging and enlightened firms.

Tom has presented scientific papers to audiences around the world; he
is recognized for his strong verbal and written communication skills, and
his ability to think differently, inspiring those around him. His personal

and business travels have also taken him to every province in Canada, as well as to Nunavut. He has worked in Canada, Venezuela, Barbados, and China and has travelled extensively for business and pleasure in Malaysia, Thailand, Singapore, China, the United States, the United Kingdom, France, Germany, the Netherlands, United Arab Emirates, Qatar, Saint Lucia, Jamaica, Turks and Caicos Islands, The Bahamas, Dominican Republic, Saint Kitts and Nevis, Mexico, Costa Rica, Colombia, and New Zealand.

Tom grew up in Toronto, Ontario, and currently lives in St. Catharines, Ontario, a short distance from Niagara Falls. He is endlessly curious, and he's passionate about helping others to fulfill their potential. Tom can be reached at tom@colucentadvisors.com.